W9-CEI-193

HOW TO DO ARCHAEOLOGY THE RIGHT WAY

Barbara A. Purdy

HOW TO DO

 # ARCHAEOLOGY

THE RIGHT WAY

UNIVERSITY PRESS OF FLORIDA

GAINESVILLE TALLAHASSEE TAMPA BOCA RATON

PENSACOLA ORLANDO MIAMI JACKSONVILLE

Copyright 1996 by the Board of Regents of the State of Florida
Printed in the United States of America on acid-free paper
All rights reserved

00 99 98 97 96   6 5 4 3 2 1

Library of Congress Cataloging-in-Publication Data
Purdy, Barbara A.
How to do archaeology the right way / Barbara A. Purdy.
p. cm.
Includes bibliographical references (p.) and index.
ISBN 0-8130-1392-5
1. Archaeology—Methodology. I. Title.
CC75.P87 1996
930.1'028—dc20 95-38050

The University Press of Florida is the scholarly publishing agency for the State University
System of Florida, comprised of Florida A & M University, Florida Atlantic University,
Florida International University, Florida State University, University of Central Florida,
University of Florida, University of North Florida, University of South Florida, and
University of West Florida.

University Press of Florida
15 Northwest 15th Street
Gainesville, FL 32611

To Hank

For always being there

CONTENTS

FIGURES

PREFACE

When people learn that I am an archaeologist, many of them say, "How exciting! I always wanted to be an archaeologist." Why do they say that? Most of the time, archaeology is not exciting at all. It is tedious, time-consuming, underfunded work often carried out under field conditions where there is no way to stay clean or to become clean after you get dirty (see frontispiece). There is danger of bug bites, snakes bites, bad weather, bad food, and, sometimes, bad company. You long for an indoor bathroom, a hot shower, a good book, and a sturdy roof over your head. After the fieldwork come weeks, months, or years of sorting, analyzing, and interpreting in order to write an article for publication that often gets turned down. In addition—though saving the world's heritage is a worthwhile and often difficult task—archaeologists are usually not paid as well as some other professionals.

What then is the attraction of archaeology? It is learning something new about something old. For example, there is nothing quite like holding a 10,000-year-old stone spearhead in your hand and trying to recreate how and why it was made and how it was used. Today, some people still hunt and go to war, but they use different kinds of weapons that are usually made of metal. Metals suitable for tool making were virtually unknown in this part of the world (the Western Hemisphere) until Europeans arrived a few hundred years ago. Even in the Old World the technology associated with metallurgy had not been in common use for very long. As soon as metals, particularly iron, became known to the Native Americans, they began to abandon the use of stone and began to use metal that they obtained through trade or by stripping metal from shipwrecks off their coasts. Today, there are very few individuals who know how to knap flint material and shape it into tools. And that is also why people are fascinated with chipped stone implements. They learn that people in the past solved problems similar to ours but in different ways. They learn something new about something old.

My reasons for writing this book, however, are not to interest you in spearheads alone but to make you aware of the information that the past holds if the proper techniques are used to recover it. Too often people collect only stone spearheads or vandalize Native American burial mounds for ceremonial pottery (hence the term **pothunters**). They do not notice what else was present, such as small flint flakes, pottery **sherds**, animal bones, and plant remains, or the type of soil, the depth of the find, and much more. Without these observations, our view of the way of life of ancient societies remains very narrow.

Many answers about the past are "blowing in the wind," and some will remain that way, but by asking the right questions and using the right methods, archaeologists come close to repeopling the ancient landscapes. That is why archaeologists do archaeology.

After first examining Florida artifacts and the lifestyles of people who made them, I will attempt to answer a question that is often asked: How does the archaeologist know where to dig? You will be surprised at how complicated the answer is to that question as well as to others, such as, Why does the archaeologist wish to excavate this particular site? In between these two questions—that is, from the time a site is discovered until excavation actually takes place—there are usually months of planning, surveying, mapping, testing, raising money, obtaining permits, and, most important of all, justifying the time and expense involved in conducting a formal investigation. The responsible archaeologist, but not the pothunter, also considers the possibility that the balance of nature will be upset by excavating an extensive area. These matters are taken up in chapter 2. Other chapters include discussion of analysis, dating, preservation, and rules and regulations.

The do's and do not's of archaeology that will be discussed in this book include:

Do:
Notify and work with a professional archaeologist if you find a site.
Excavate systematically.
Collect everything.

Record everything.

Take pictures.

Learn the age of the artifacts you have excavated.

Learn how your site fits into what is already known.

Do not:

Collect objects without the property owner's permission.

Just dig holes.

Collect only spearheads, pottery bowls, and ornaments.

Dig unmarked burial sites, such as Indian burial mounds.

Separate objects from their context without good records.

Collect objects for your pleasure alone. (Archaeology belongs to the citizens of the state, the country, and the world. Keeping these things yourself would be like a scientist finding a cure for cancer but not publicizing his discovery. Everyone loses.)

Most of the sites and artifacts discussed and illustrated in this book come from Florida, but the excavation techniques and analyses described can be applied worldwide. Boldfaced terms in the text are defined in a glossary at the back of the volume.

ACKNOWLEDGMENTS

I have been "doing" and/or teaching Florida archaeology since 1967, but I was amazed at how much I did not know when I began to write various sections of this book. I am particularly grateful to Brent R. Weisman for his advice on numerous occasions. He always called me back when I needed to ask him a question. I thank Lani K. Friend for excellent editorial suggestions. Various individuals in the Division of Historical Resources, Florida Department of State, were very cooperative in supplying me with the latest publications about rules and regulations governing Florida antiquities: James J. Miller, Marion Smith, Roger C. Smith, and Louis D. Tesar. I thank Glen H. Doran for his generosity in permitting me to use data and pictures from the Windover site; Marion S. Gilliland for photographs of Key Marco artifacts; and Alvin Hendrix of McIntosh for allowing me to photograph specimens from his collections. Pictures and illustrations not credited following the caption were produced or reproduced specifically for this volume. As always, I am deeply appreciative of the continuing assistance of the Florida Museum of Natural History staff and curators. I thank Ann S. Cordell, Elise LeCompte Baer, J. T.

Milanich, and Elizabeth S. Wing for their efforts on my behalf. I owe a debt to all those colleagues and associates who have influenced my thinking throughout the years, in direct communication and through their works. Although many of these people are not included in my list of works cited, all deserve credit for the contribution this book may make. I accept full responsibility for its deficiencies.

ONE

ARTIFACTS AND THE
LIFESTYLES OF THE PEOPLE
WHO MADE THEM

In any scientific endeavor, interpretations are modified when new data are collected. The story that follows is as accurate as the information available at this time. It represents a synopsis of the evidence about the state's ancient inhabitants compiled from thousands of archaeological sites for more than 150 years. The presentation of this accumulated knowledge should convince the reader of the richness of Florida's cultural heritage.

Classification, or **typology**, is absolutely essential to describe the universe as an orderly place. Classification is a convenience tool that can be as simple or as complex as is necessary to reduce phenomena of any kind to categories that make sense and can be understood. For instance, we classify dogs into the animal kingdom and distinguish them from other animals based on various characteristics that we recognize when we see them again. Some **taxonomists** are "lumpers" and others are "splitters." "Lumpers" would place all dogs in a single category no matter how different one dog looks from another, and they would be basically correct in doing so. "Splitters" would separate poodles from Great Danes, bulldogs from Dobermans, etc., and they also would be basically correct in doing so.

Artifacts are objects made or used by people for a multitude of reasons. The more complex a society becomes, the more items are needed to do all of the things required for the culture to function correctly. In Florida, before the coming of Europeans, the native peoples made artifacts from stone, bone, wood, shell, clays (**ceramics**), and plant fibers (textiles). No metals are native to Florida, but a few artifacts made of copper have been recovered at Florida sites. These items were imported from elsewhere in the Southeast. Gold, silver, iron, glass, and nonnative ceramics occur at sites that date more recently than A.D. 1492. They were probably obtained from shipwrecks or through trade and distributed by the Indians throughout the state.

Artifacts usually can be classified by shape, design, function, and material. Obviously, if you can classify an artifact using all four of these characteristics, your interpretation about where it fits into the archaeology of an area is more secure. Stone spearheads can be described by shape, material, and assumed function (hunting or warfare). Some artifacts must be classified using fewer characteristics. For example, we know that the function of a stone hammer is to pound, but we can only guess at what it pounded. Since its shape or style does not change much through time, it is difficult to assign it to a specific time period unless other information is available, such as associated diagnostic artifacts or organic material that can be dated by radiocarbon analysis. Another example is the ulna awl made from one of the bones of the foreleg of a deer or other animal. This artifact **type** was made for thousands of years. When reading the following pages, keep in mind that classification is imposed on the objects being described to create order. This categorization does not always reflect reality; that is, it does not necessarily reflect what the maker had in mind when the artifact was manufactured or used thousands of years ago.

In this chapter, I describe and picture the artifacts created and/or used by native Floridians from the very earliest evidence until after the **Contact period**. These stages or periods of occupation in Florida can also be classified. They are called **Paleoindian** (before 10,000 to about 9000 B.P.), **Archaic** (9000–4000 B.P.), **Ceramic**, sometimes called **Formative** (4000–500 B.P.), and **Early Historic** (500–300 B.P.). B.P. stands for "before present" and is defined in chapter 4. By about A.D. 1700 the original Florida Indians had been virtually wiped out, and Indians from the North, known later as the **Seminoles**, moved into the void created by their absence.

The word *stage* to archaeologists implies a way of life, while the word *period* usually refers to time. The Paleoindian period, for example, is considered a big-game-hunting stage, and the Archaic period is usually thought of as a stage when rapid adjustments to new **ecological** conditions took place following the retreat of the glaciers after the last ice age. Actually, most archaeologists use the terms *period* and *stage* interchangeably.

PALEOINDIAN PERIOD

The Paleoindian period can be divided into three phases: Early, Middle, and Late. These divisions are probably significant, as I will try to demonstrate, but a great deal more work needs to be done. Practically no chronometric dates exist for the Early Paleoindian period in Florida, and nearly all surviving diagnostic artifacts from this period are made of stone. The evidence for antiquity, therefore, is based on the comparative method as described in chapter 4; that is, we assume that certain artifacts in Florida are contemporaneous with those from other areas that have been securely dated because their shapes are nearly identical. It should be noted that nearly all of the choice specimens are in the possession of amateur collectors, whose cooperation was essential in compiling the story that follows.

Early Paleoindian

The Clovis point (fig. 1.1) is a characteristic stone artifact from the Early Paleoindian phase. In the western United States this type of point has been found in association with extinct elephants (mammoths and mastodons) (fig.

1.1. Florida Clovis points. (From the Alvin Hendrix collection.)

1.2. (a) Mammoth; (b) mastodon. (Courtesy of S. David Webb.)

1.2). The sites from which they have been recovered are approximately 11,000 to 11,400 years old. In Florida, dozens of Clovis points have been recovered from rivers and springs, but none has been found in association with extinct animals or in association with materials that can be dated by radiocarbon analysis. But here is where the archaeologist plays detective and begins to build a logical case for their contemporaneity with the western finds.

1. The Clovis point is very distinctive stylistically, and this style is not found anywhere in the Western Hemisphere during any time other than the Early Paleoindian phase.

2. In Florida, elephant ivory was fashioned into tools (fig. 1.3). About 40 of these tools have been found (Webb 1994). Since the ivory can be worked only when it is fresh, it is logical to conclude that people and elephants were living in Florida at the same time. Limited evidence (at present) suggests that

1.3. Elephant tusk artifact and close-up of zigzag lines. (Courtesy of C. Vance Haynes, Jr.)

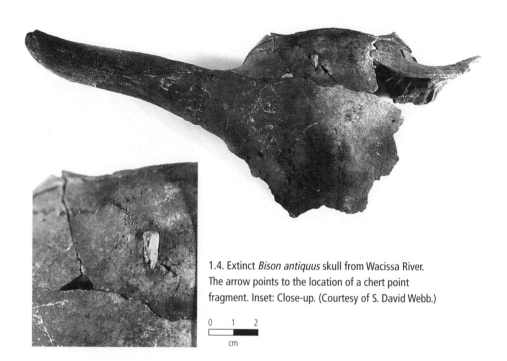

1.4. Extinct *Bison antiquus* skull from Wacissa River. The arrow points to the location of a chert point fragment. Inset: Close-up. (Courtesy of S. David Webb.)

0   1   2
cm

the Pleistocene megafauna of Florida became extinct about 10,000 B.P.; therefore, the ivory tools must be older than 10,000 years.

3. In addition to the ivory tools, bones of several extinct animals, including mammoths and mastodons, ancient bison (*Bison antiquus*), and a giant land tortoise (*Geochelone crassiscutata*) have been found that appear to have been killed by humans, and some of these bones bear traces of butchering marks. An 11,000-year-old bison from the Wacissa River was found with a fragment of an unidentifiable stone spearhead embedded in its skull (fig. 1.4). A butchered mastodon tusk from the Aucilla River was dated at more than 12,000 years old; organic materials found in association were used for the radiocarbon analysis. A giant land tortoise with a burned carapace, recovered from a ledge now 26 meters underwater at Little Salt Spring, apparently was impaled by a wooden spear that was dated at 12,030 B.P. The butchered mastodon tusk and the tortoise are both older than the oldest western Clovis finds, but they are missing the diagnostic Clovis point. Technically, then, they could be considered pre-Clovis or pre-Early Paleoindian, but this topic has not been addressed.

1.5. Bola stones. (From the Alvin Hendrix collection.)

4. The styles of the Middle and Late Paleoindian spearheads in Florida differ quite significantly from Clovis points.

5. At the present time Clovis points have not been found at any of Florida's stone quarries used by early Floridians. This fact suggests that Clovis people in Florida were not permanent residents (they were "tourists," or the first "snow birds") and that they brought with them an already fashioned tool kit made of nonlocal materials. This theory can be proved only by using complex instruments and trained technicians to conduct compositional analysis of the suspected imports and comparing the results of these analyses against a "fingerprint" of Florida cherts (see chapter 3). There is some support for the above statement. The **bola stone** (fig. 1.5) is an artifact that has been found in some of Florida's rivers in locations where Paleoindian materials also occur. To my knowledge, it has not been found at terrestrial sites along with more recent materials. The bola stone is usually made from a river-rounded cobble that has been modified. It looks like a hen's egg that has a shallow indentation in the smaller end. It closely resembles specimens used by the Eskimos and native peoples of Patagonia that are tied with thongs, knotted at the indentation, and thrown to ensnare the legs of running animals or flying birds (fig. 1.6). The important aspect is that the bola stone is usually made of stone material that is not native to Florida. It follows, then, that many of the Paleoindian points could be made of nonlocal material also.

1.6. Bola stones thrown to bring down an animal (based on pictures of Gauchos and Eskimos using a similar technique).

To summarize, the Early Paleoindian period in Florida is tantalizing to think about, but absolute proof of its presence still lies just beyond our reach.

Middle and Late Paleoindian

There is no question about the existence of the Middle and Late phases of the Paleoindian period in Florida. Hundreds of Middle and Late Paleoindian spearheads have been found. These phases will be considered together since it is impossible to separate them chronologically at present, and there is some limited evidence that they may have coexisted.

The major styles of spearheads from the Middle Paleoindian phase are the Suwannee and Simpson (fig. 1.7). From the Late Paleoindian phase the primary stone point is the Bolen (fig. 1.8). There are numerous other types that can be assigned to each of these phases but they are not common.

As mentioned above, chronometric dates are scarce for the entire Paleoindian period in Florida, but there is some indication that only modern **fauna** survived in Florida by the Late Paleoindian phase and probably even earlier during the Middle Paleoindian phase, i.e., about 10,000 years ago. The best clues for this claim come from the Little Salt Spring site in Sarasota County and the Page-Ladson site in Jefferson County. At Little Salt Spring, dates of 9900–9600 B.P. were obtained from artifacts (wooden stakes) and botanical remains, all in association with modern fauna, recovered from the 12-meter sloping basin surrounding the opening to the lower cavern (fig. 1.9). Unfortunately, no diagnostic stone implements were found, but at the Page-Ladson site a Bolen point was recovered from a stratum that was dated at 9730±120

A   B

1.7. (a) Suwannee points; (b) Simpson points. (From the Alvin Hendrix collection.)

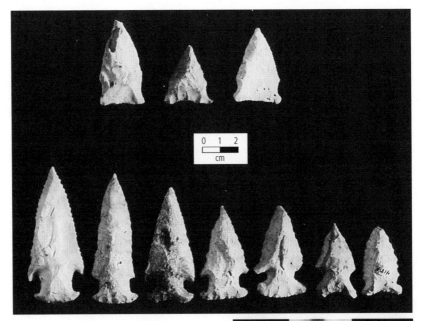

1.8. Stone points of the Late Paleoindian period. The Bolen point shown in the bottom row is the style most commonly found in Florida and is often beveled (inset).

1.9. Little Salt Spring, showing the location of excavations adjacent to the opening to the lower cavern. (From Purdy 1991.)

B.P. All of the associated fauna were modern species. In addition, wherever extinct animals occur in undisturbed contexts, they are embedded in geological strata that differ significantly from the strata in which all modern fauna are found.

As mentioned above, there is some evidence that there is little or no reason to divide the Middle and Late Paleoindian phases temporally. At the Harney Flats site in Hillsborough County, Suwannee, Simpson (Middle Paleoindian), and Bolen (Late Paleoindian) points were found together, well sealed from more recent Archaic styles by a 20-cm thick **hardpan** stratum. Unfortunately, no animal bones or other organic materials were available for dating. It is possible that there are no age differences between the Middle and Late Paleoindian phases, but it is also possible that the points ended up in the same stratum because of a lack of **deposition** of **sediments** that would separate one phase from the other. In other words, **erosion** may have exceeded deposition and mixed materials that were temporally distinct. Since Harney Flats is the only site in Florida that has furnished this kind of stratigraphy, it is impossible to draw conclusions. It should be noted, however, that from a stone quarry site excavated in the 1970s, Bolen points were found in association with Early-Middle Archaic points (see below), indicating that erosion had exceeded deposition at that site, mixing the deposits. At any rate, the combined Middle and Late Paleoindian phases probably did not last more than 1,000 years.

In addition to the distinctive spearhead styles described above, the rest of the Paleoindian tool kit is also unique. It consists of exquisite **unifacial** blades, knives, scrapers, and other objects of various sizes, shapes, and areas of use (i.e., blades, side scrapers, end scrapers, gravers, etc.), always with steep edge angles that probably resulted from resharpening (fig. 1.10). These implements are small and lightweight, reflecting a nomadic existence in which a portable, flexible tool kit was essential. They were used to skin animals, prepare hides, make spear shafts, and much more. For many years in North America this

1.10. Paleoindian tool kit. These specimens are all unifacial (flaked only on one side) except the two on the top and middle left. (From Purdy 1981.)

distinctive tool kit has been recognized as being associated with the Paleoindian period or a big game hunting way of life. Beautifully made blade tools in particular are considered the hallmark of the Paleoindian period. These kinds of stone tools are found in rivers and springs in Florida, but it was not until the Harney Flats site was excavated that they could be connected definitely with Florida's Middle-Late Paleoindian phases and probably also with the Early Paleoindian phase. As we shall see, these nicely made implements contrast sharply with Archaic period tools. It is interesting to note also that many of these unifacial Paleoindian tools look exactly like types that were made in Europe more than 10,000 years ago.

In addition to the stone remains and the elephant ivory implements already mentioned, socketed bone or antler points appear to be another Paleoindian tool. They are found in rivers and streams often in areas where Paleoindian stone points are recovered. Although similar specimens have been recovered, such as those from the Windover site, to my knowledge the typical socketed points of the Paleoindian period have not been recovered from a terrestrial site along with more recent materials. They were presumably used as weapons or tools with the socketed portions fitted onto wooden handles or cane shafts, none of which has survived or has been recognized as modified.

Another clue to the antiquity of certain nondiagnostic bone and stone tools should be mentioned. The waters of some rivers, such as the Santa Fe in northern Florida, have a high mineral content that gradually discolors objects deposited in them. The Paleoindian points that have been found in these highly mineralized waters tend to be black, whereas points of more recent date are either brown (Archaic period) or have hardly changed color at all, depending on how old they are. When bones and other stone tools are found in the same area and are also black, it probably can be concluded that they are the same age as the Paleoindian points. It is entirely possible that scientific methods could be developed to determine the rate of mineralization or **fossilization** of these remains, but this research has not been conducted.

In conclusion, the Paleoindian period was a time when nomadic big game hunters entered Florida chasing animals, some of which are now extinct. It is probably true that the Paleoindian people did much more than merely hunt, but the evidence for other activities is not available. They may have come to Florida to enjoy a milder climate at a time when glacial ice still covered a large part of the North American continent. Florida was essentially a desert during this time period because much of the world's water supply was tied up in glaciers during the last ice age. The vegetation that we see around us today did not exist. Most of the rivers did not flow. The ocean was a hundred meters lower than it is now, which means that Florida's coasts extended much farther east, west, and south. The large animals sought by the Paleoindian people may have been attracted to the extensive grasslands that occurred in areas now underwater or covered with pine forest.

ARCHAIC PERIOD

About 10,000 years ago the world's climate began to change quite rapidly from Ice Age conditions to those we recognize today. Sea level rose dramatically, **inundating** former coastlines. Areas that had once enjoyed rather wet conditions, such as the Sahara Desert and the American Southwest, began to dry up. On the other hand, the interior upland of Florida changed from a desertlike landscape with very little surface water to one of rivers, ponds, and lush vegetation. For reasons not fully understood, many Ice Age animals became extinct at this time. Extinctions occurred worldwide and included not only animals hunted by humans but many other species as well. Human groups who depended upon the Pleistocene megafauna for a major source of food had to modify their lifeways to adjust to the new conditions.

Thus emerged the Archaic way of life, which lasted throughout North America from about 9,000 years ago until at least 4,500 years ago; in some locations it still existed when Indian groups were first contacted by Europeans in the sixteenth century. The Archaic implies more than a time period; it refers to a stage of human adaptation that began with the need for rapid adjustments to changing ecological conditions at the end of the last ice age. Continued refinement of knowledge about plant and animal habitats and development of technologies to exploit these resources efficiently led to a very effective way of life for many human groups throughout the Americas.

The Archaic is sometimes called a stage of "total exploitation," during which people took advantage of everything edible or usable in the environment. This may have been true in some areas or at times of great stress, but it does not appear to be typical. Certain foods provided greater return for the effort needed to gather and process them. These foods became the **staples** that were utilized most often while other potential products were ignored. Thus, as time passed, the archaeological record of the Eastern Woodlands reveals that deer, fish, shellfish, and nuts (acorn, hickory) were probably the food items most exploited. Total exploitation may have been a traditional practice where environmental conditions were not so lush; for example, the American South-west.

The introduction of the **spearthrower,** or **atlatl** (an Aztec word) (figs. 1.11 and 1.12), into the Eastern Woodlands may have been the stimulus for the change in stone point styles that occurs. The stone points from the Early Ar-chaic through the Middle Archaic tend to average larger than those of the Paleoindian period. The atlatl was an important technological advance. With it the spear could be thrown farther and with greater force and accuracy than with the unaided arm. It was usually of "composite manufacture consisting of a wooden shaft, often with a weight mounted toward the center of the shaft for balance, and a handle with finger loops" (Jennings 1989).

A significant new cultural practice was initiated during either Late Paleo-indian or Early Archaic times. Flintworkers discovered that by heating Florida **chert** very carefully to 350°C and allowing it to cool slowly beneficial changes were imparted to the stone that facilitated **flaking** and produced a more aes-thetically pleasing implement. The heating process reduces the point tensile strength of the stone by nearly 50 percent, resulting in a material that is much easier to flake and has a sharper edge. In addition, the stone often turns from

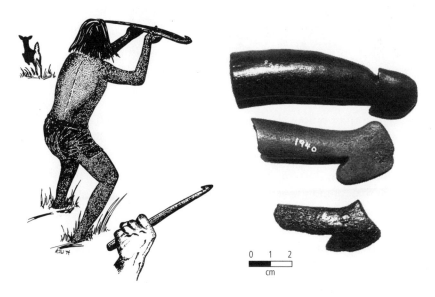

1.11. Atlatl, or spearthrower (method of use based on speculation).

1.12. Atlatl hooks. (From the Alvin Hendrix collection.)

1.13. Experimental specimens showing color change when Florida chert is heated slowly.

0 1 2
cm

1.14. Examples of heat-altered Early and Middle Archaic chert bifaces (spearheads or lance-heads). Vitreous luster occurs when specimens are flaked after the material is heated.

beige/brown to various shades of pink/red depending upon its iron content (shown left to right in fig. 1.13). A vitreous luster appears when a specimen is flaked into its final form following the heating procedure (fig. 1.14). When the impurities within the interstitial spaces of the randomly oriented micro-crystals that compose the structure of chert reach a melting point during heating, the microcrystals are fitted more closely together (see chapter 3). Thus a material is created that fractures more like glass and has a greater reflective value upon subsequent flaking (the vitreous luster) (Purdy and Brooks 1971).

This new procedure was a bonanza to flintworkers, who had to manufacture implements from Florida chert, which tends to be very tough and fossiliferous. At any rate, by the Early Archaic period most projectile points had been subjected to the heat treating process and usually can be distinguished by their color and shiny appearance. Very few other stone implements, such as hammerstones, would benefit from heat alteration because the material becomes brittle and shatters easily. Studies have shown that heat treatment was applied primarily to **preformed** projectile points.

As with the Paleoindian period, the Florida Archaic has been divided into three phases: Early, about 9000–7000 B.P.; Middle, about 7000–5500 B.P.; and Late, about 5500–4000 B.P. It should be noted, however, that neither the chronology nor the cultural differences of these three phases are well established and that conclusions about their existence are often based on findings from a single site.

Until the 1970s and 1980s, the Archaic period in Florida was known primarily for its thousands of stone spearheads. Other stone implements found with the spearheads were not very interesting or diagnostic. The sites where these stone remains were recovered usually consisted of about a foot (30 cm) of sandy soil with no visual geologic or cultural differences throughout this shallow deposit. No organic material was preserved because the soil was well drained and because the acid pH destroyed the bone (pH, or hydrogen power, is a symbol for acidity or alkalinity; pH values from 0 to 7 indicate acid conditions, and those from 7 to 14 indicate alkaline conditions). The entire 5,000-year period was essentially neglected, and it almost seems as if people mentally collapsed this long time span into a year of human activity. Now, as a result of modern development in Florida, a number of archaeological wet sites have been found that date to the Archaic period. They are providing exciting new knowledge about Archaic lifeways.

Archaeological wet sites are located in permanently saturated, oxygen-free deposits that entomb and preserve organic objects that seldom survive elsewhere. Specific Florida wet sites will be discussed in the following paragraphs.

Early Archaic

The most common stone spearhead from the Early Archaic in Florida is the Kirk Serrated (fig. 1.15). It differs significantly from the Paleoindian styles. It has been recovered from numerous terrestrial sites as well as from rivers and springs. Nevertheless, until the Windover site was excavated, documentation of its antiquity was based on the comparative method by noting similarities to points recovered from securely dated sites throughout the rest of the southeastern United States. At the Windover site, Kirk Serrated points were associated with organic materials that were dated from about 7,000 to more than 8,000 years old. The points probably arrived at the site in already finished

1.15. Kirk Serrated (on right) and other point types of the Early Archaic in Florida. (From Purdy 1981.)

form because chert material does not occur locally in that area of Florida (Brevard County).

Windover is a landmark site (fig. 1.16). It not only has placed the Kirk Serrated squarely in the time frame where it was believed to belong but it also has revealed an abundance of information about plants and animals that were utilized for food and fiber, human burial activities, and physical attributes (including age at death and pathologies) of the people interred in a 7,000- to 8,000-year-old cemetery in Florida. It has provided insights about cultural

1.16. Excavations in progress at the Windover site, Brevard County, Florida. The site was totally submerged but was kept dry by using a dewatering system and a rotary diesel pump. In other words, the people in this picture would be underwater if the pump were turned off. (Courtesy of Glen H. Doran.)

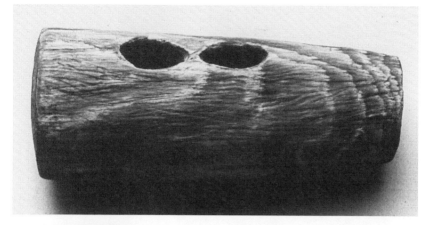

1.17. Wood artifact from the Windover site. Although the function is not known, it has been called a "whistle" because of the holes placed lengthwise and at each end (inset). Wood species is pine. (Courtesy of Glen H. Doran.)

1.18. Heavy twined fabric from the Windover site. (Courtesy of Glen H. Doran.)

practices that were not known before at this time depth for the entire North American continent. The site has been described in great detail by Doran and Dickel (1988) and Purdy (1991) and in numerous technical articles.

The stone artifacts recovered from the Windover site were such a small part of the total **assemblage** that, had they been the only specimens excavated, the site would not have been considered very significant. The overwhelming majority of all materials from the site were of organic composition. These included wooden artifacts (fig. 1.17), textiles (fig. 1.18), incised bone objects, deer antler tools, **floral** and faunal remains, and 168 human burials, 91 of which had brain tissue preserved in the **crania**. Textiles included

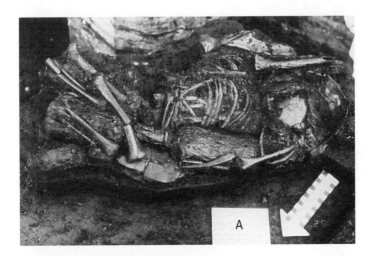

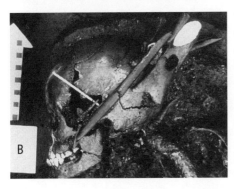

1.19. Human burials at the Windover site: (a) 7,000–8,000-year-old child burial accompanied by numerous grave goods, including a turtle carapace, bone artifacts, and a double-ended pestle made of oak; (b) 7,000–8,000-year-old adult burial. Note the bone and drilled antler artifacts. The white object in the upper right of the picture is a stone spearhead. The thin white object was used to prop up an artifact. (Courtesy of Glen H. Doran.)

bags, hoods, blankets, and clothing using several types of weaving designs. No other textiles have been found in Florida, and it is not until the introduction of pottery about 4,000 years ago that examples of textile designs reappear. (Apparently the natives would place the still pliable clay on mats to shape it into pots. At least 12 different kinds of weaving patterns have been identified from pot bottoms throughout the state.)

Another significant aspect of the Windover site is that grave goods were recovered from child burials. It has been generally believed that children would not be accorded special attention in death unless they were the sons or daughters of chiefs whose status was inherited and whose offspring would eventually take over the position. The people at Windover must represent an egalitarian society, yet many of the children found in the cemetery were buried with grave goods (fig. 1.19). It probably can be concluded that the parents, as parents everywhere, grieved over the death of their young ones and sent their prized possessions with them to the afterworld.

As mentioned above, Windover is the only site in the Americas that has supplied detailed information about certain cultural practices, artifacts, and human populations dating to the Early Archaic. There are, however, other sites in the southeastern United States where stone and some bone artifacts have been recovered in good stratigraphic sequences. These sites have shown that Early Archaic stone tools, other than spearheads, remained quite similar to those of the Paleoindians. They have also revealed that only modern fauna existed by 9,000 to 10,000 years ago, and that people were utilizing deer and smaller game and were consuming an abundance of hickory nuts and other plant foods.

The Early Archaic period lasted for about 2,000 years. I consider it a time of transition from the Paleoindian big game hunting, nomadic way of life to the more localized, sedentary life style of the Middle Archaic that followed.

Middle Archaic

The Middle Archaic has been known traditionally for its Christmas tree–shaped stone projectile points (fig. 1.20a). The rest of the **chipped stone** industry from the Middle Archaic was not well described until I excavated two quarry sites in Central Florida in the 1970s. These sites yielded thousands of stone remains that dated principally to the Archaic period. They permitted me to document quite precisely the step-by-step process of projectile point manufacture because at quarries many failures are discarded at various stages of completion. But other activities were taking place at the quarry besides spearhead production.

The reader should attempt to imagine an area with tremendous quantities of flint rock utilized by only small groups at a time over several thousand years. There was material to waste and it apparently was wasted. This fact may be sad news for environmentalists who believe that people in the past did not squander irreplaceable resources, but it is a bonanza for archaeologists because it makes it possible to study large collections and to begin to draw some conclusions about how the quarries were used.

Observations made at quarry workshop sites indicate that heavy utilization of Florida chert occurred during the Early and Middle Archaic periods. Paradoxically, except for a wide variety of projectile points and some stemmed end scrapers and drills made from broken projectile points, the greatest majority of the stone implements found at Archaic quarry sites in Florida cannot

1.20. (a) Newnans point and (b) chipped stone tool kit of the Middle Archaic. (From Purdy 1981.)

be classified into distinct categories based on style or discrete function. Unlike the sophisticated tools of the Paleoindian period, many of these implements are large, appear to have been used for a variety of tasks, and have a shape that seems to have resulted from use rather than an intentional process of manufacture.

This observation permits tentative conclusions about the Florida Archaic way of life, particularly in the central highlands. The people either lived close to the quarries or the quarries were visited as part of a seminomadic lifestyle. Since stone is heavy, materials needing stone in order to be fashioned into artifacts were brought to the quarry instead of quarried stone being brought to a camp site. Thus the quarries became industrial sites where a variety of articles were made. It is possible to speculate that activities other than projectile point manufacture included the production of canoes, clubs, spear and arrow shafts, basketry, religious items, works of art, etc. A full range of stone utilization is found at outcrop workshop sites, including hammers, choppers to cut down trees, a variety of adzes and scrapers to shape wood and bone, and burins used to make incisions on materials such as animal hides and human skin (fig 1.20b). If quarries were visited frequently, it is quite possible that the same stone **debitage** could be used again and again for a variety of tasks until it was exhausted, thus obscuring its original function. Another important observation is that quarries were used to teach young people how to work flint. Symmetry and uniformity of flake removal are essential for the production of stone spearheads, and yet specimens were examined where flaking was crude and symmetry was not maintained.

It can be argued that the kinds of stone remains from quarry sites would differ significantly from those found at camp or village sites, but the fact is

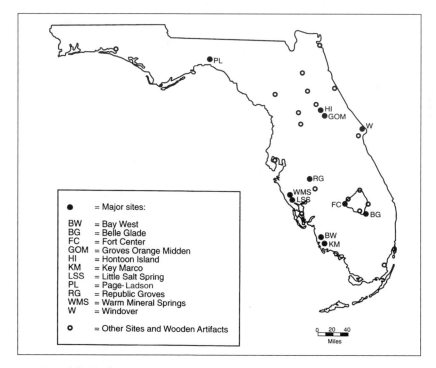

1.21. Map of Florida showing major water-saturated archaeological sites.

that the stone remains that have been studied from camp sites tend to verify the fact that there are very few diagnostic stone implements other than projectile points during the Middle Archaic period.

There are four sites in Florida that have furnished more extensive information than that provided by stone about cultural activities dating from approximately 6,500 to 6,000 B.P. Little Salt Spring, Bay West, Republic Groves, and Gauthier (fig. 1.21) are Middle to Late Archaic cemeteries where, except at the Gauthier site, bodies were interred in waterlogged organic deposits as at Windover. Human burials have survived in excellent condition, as have the usually perishable grave goods that accompanied them. These include woven objects used as shrouds; wood, bone, and antler artifacts (fig. 1.22); and botanical remains such as bottle gourds. It appears that the bodies were staked down at the Little Salt Spring and Republic Groves sites. Human brains were preserved in the crania of individuals from the Little Salt Spring and Repub-

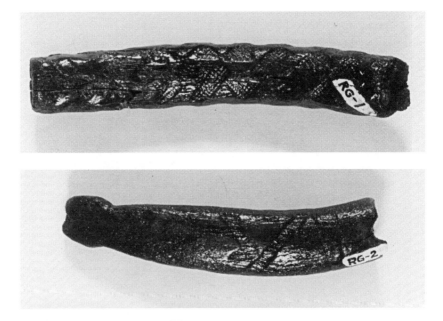

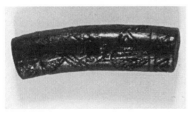

1.22. Incised antler artifacts from the Republic Groves site. (From Purdy 1991.)

lic Grove sites and possibly from the Bay West site as well. Studies of physical attributes have been conducted on the skeletons from the Little Salt Spring, Republic Grove, Bay West, and, partially, the Gauthier sites. These studies have supplied information about age at death, sex and age distribution in the cemetery, pathologies, injuries, nutrition, and much more. Gauthier differs from the waterlogged sites because the human skeletons (approximately 110 of them) were interred in a wet sand deposit, and the bones became mineralized because of the saturated soil conditions. Bone and antler artifacts but no botanical specimens survived at the Gauthier site.

Rather extensive radiocarbon dating has been done of all of these sites except Gauthier. In addition, typical Middle Archaic stone points were found at all of the sites. Newnans points, in particular, provide a good marker for the period. This nicely made point was named for a site at Newnans Lake in Alachua County and was securely dated at that site. Other artifacts found at the cemetery sites include polished stone axes, celts, ornaments, and beads made of marine shell and nonlocal stone. This fact, of course, indicates that Florida was not completely isolated from contact with other cultures. Most of the Middle Archaic waterlogged sites were discovered during development projects; thus, the original **provenience** of the artifacts was lost. One can have confidence in the 6500–6000 B.P. dates, however, because the water-saturated mortuary sites appear to be **single component** and most of them have yielded well-preserved organic materials that have been dated by radiocarbon analysis.

The custom of burying people in moist depressions or ponds ceased around 6,000 years ago. Since people are slow to change the way they treat the dead, it is interesting to speculate about the events that might have stimulated a change in burial practices.

Sometime toward the end of the Middle Archaic period, people became more and more efficient at exploiting marine and freshwater shellfish, fish, and turtles, all of which were becoming plentiful as modern conditions in Florida began to emerge. Implements and ornaments made from large marine conch shells began to appear.

Late Archaic

The term *late* implies the end of a period or the beginning of something new. Major changes in cultural orientation, many initiated in the latter part of the Middle Archaic, occurred during this last phase of prehistory before ceramics are introduced into Florida.

The Groves Orange Midden site (also known as the Enterprise site) is a waterlogged site on the north shore of Lake Monroe that has produced a nearly complete and unlimited assemblage of environmental and cultural "trash." It has provided hitherto unknown insights into environment and diet along the St. Johns River during the Middle to Late Archaic.

The large chert quarries in the central highland area were rarely utilized after the Middle Archaic. This statement is based on results of excavations at the Senator Edwards and the Container Corporation of America sites, both in Marion County, where hundreds of Early to Middle Archaic points were recovered, but more recently dated points were seldom found. At habitation sites dating to the Late Archaic, many points appear to be reworked Middle Archaic spearheads in that they are essentially the same style but stubbier and thicker. What kinds of conclusions about cultural changes can be drawn from this situation? The following comments are pure speculation at present but may hold up under rigorous testing.

When people became drawn to aquatic resources as these resources became more plentiful along the rivers and coasts, they moved away from the highland area and thus away from the large quarries. The Tampa embayment region has sources of high-quality flint materials, but no outcrops occur on the east coast or to the south. My theory is that as populations became more sedentary along, for instance, the St. Johns River, they simply reworked and reused antique stone specimens when they found them.

Another point to consider is the development of marine shell technology. Although crudely made marine shell artifacts dating 8000–7000 B.P. were recovered at the Windover site, the creation of all manner of shell tools, weapons, and ornaments seems to have blossomed during the Late Archaic and continued up to historic times. At the base of the shell midden at Lake Monroe, an extremely burned "cooking vessel" made of marine shell was dated at 5900 B.P., thus of Middle to Late Archaic age. Above this level, other types of marine shell tools and marine shell beads were recovered with dates ranging from about 5600 to 5100 B.P., still with no ceramics present. At the Crescent Beach site on the Atlantic coast, similar tools were recovered that date to approximately the same time. The problem is that at most terrestrial sites the opportunity for good stratigraphic control often does not exist or was not maintained by the excavator and that material suitable for radiocarbon dating does not survive.

For example, from the Tick Island site, located in the St. Johns River valley between Lake Dexter and Lake Woodruff, a great variety of shell tools and ornaments was found when dragline operations removed portions of the shell mound to be used for commercial reasons. It is well established that portions of this site are at least 6,000 years old, but unfortunately the materials from many time periods were mixed during the mining activities so it is difficult to say when shell technology was introduced at the site. Marine shell tools were not recovered during excavations at three Archaic sites in the Ocala National Forest. These sites dated around 5000+ B.P., but most of the dates were obtained from freshwater snail shells *(Viviparus georgianus)* and may not be as accurate as desired. When marine shell tools are found in freshwater midden deposits, as along the St. Johns River, it is certain they were brought in from the coast to be used. In contrast, at certain Gulf Coast sites where marine shells exist by the thousands, it is not always clear whether they were artifacts or were discarded after a conch feast. In South Florida, diagnostic flint tools are seldom recovered and organic materials that might be used for dating are not preserved except at water-saturated cemetery sites.

Therefore, in the absence of ceramics, good stratigraphy, or datable material, how would it be possible to know exactly when shell tool technology is added to the cultural inventory? One clue comes from the South Florida cemetery sites that are fairly securely dated to the Middle Archaic. No shell vessels, tools, or ornaments were recovered as grave goods at these sites, indicating that the technology was not yet well developed or important, although the Gauthier site farther north did produce numerous shell beads made of marine conch. Nevertheless, marine shell technology became extremely im-

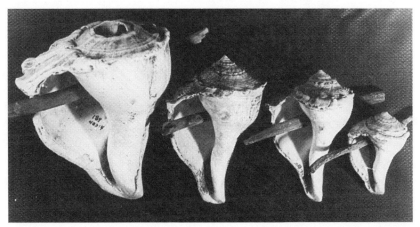

1.23. Shell tools from the Key Marco site, Collier County, Florida.
(Courtesy of Marion S. Gilliland.)

0   1   2
cm

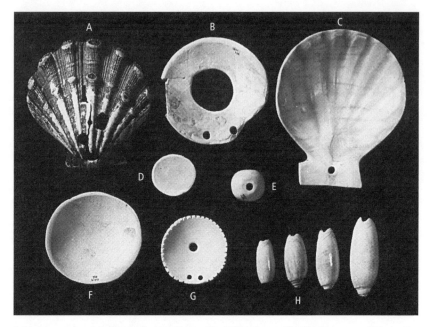

1.24. Ornaments of shell from the Key Marco site, Collier County, Florida. (Courtesy of Marion S. Gilliland.)

portant during the Late Archaic period in South Florida and in parts of North Florida, where shell was perhaps easier to procure and more versatile than flint. The greatest diversity and quantity of marine shell artifacts have been found in South Florida. As many as 60 different categories of shell objects have been described for the area (figs. 1.23 and 1.24).

The use of bone for weapons, tools, and ornaments is very ancient in Florida. Bone technology continues to develop through time, but this expansion may be more apparent than real because of larger populations and better preservation at more recent sites. Bone probably substituted for stone in places where suitable flint was not available for the manufacture of projectile points and other kinds of tools. In these locations, such as East and South Florida, bone and shell technology was well developed. Despite the great diversity of artifacts produced from these two materials, Willey (1949a:47) recognized very little overlap between the shell and bone industries and concluded that they "complemented each other in a well-adjusted pattern of use."

Decorated bone and antler have been recovered in Florida dating to the Early and Middle Archaic, and bone ornaments, particularly "pins" probably used in the hair or as a means to secure clothing, become very elaborate in more recent time periods. Most of the hundreds of bone artifacts recovered so far from Late Archaic shell midden sites are plain and utilitarian, but incised bone is known from this time period. At the Lake Monroe site, small fragments of elaborately decorated bone artifacts were recovered from and below the shell midden (fig. 1.25). Many varieties of bone ornaments were found at Tick Island, but, as mentioned above, it is not possible to determine their chronology.

In conclusion, new attributes are introduced during the Late Archaic (called Mount Taylor in the mid–St. Johns River valley) and some old practices are abandoned. Ecological conditions made it possible for people to "harvest" aquatic resources. As they learned to exploit these resources effectively through the development of new technologies or the application of old techniques to a new environment, they enjoyed a food supply as (or more) reliable than agriculture. This way of life persisted in most of Florida until the arrival of Europeans in the sixteenth century. Shell middens that eventually became huge began to grow primarily in the Late Archaic, and it seems that marine

1.25. Fragments of decorated bone artifacts from Groves Orange Midden, Volusia County, Florida. Bottom specimen was dated 6200 B.P.

shell technology was developed at this time also. Ceramics have not yet appeared but clay "boiling" balls are present. Greater cultural complexity is evident in Florida by 4500 B.P., but it is difficult to place emphasis on a single component, other than increased use of aquatic resources, to account for this complexity. It is possible that larger populations or external stimuli from neighboring cultures were prime movers for cultural change.

CERAMIC PERIOD

Some scholars say the lifestyles of the Archaic period in peninsular Florida persisted to the time of early contact around A.D. 1500. And they would probably be correct because the Archaic lifestyle seems to have remained in most locations in the peninsula until the Europeans arrived. This was not the case for the Panhandle region of Florida nor for the rest of the southeastern United States, where horticulture was introduced quite early. In some places it became an important if not dominating way to control the food supply, especially after A.D. 1000 when *Zea maize* (corn) became a major subsistence item.

I have chosen to differentiate between the Archaic and the Ceramic periods because (1) ceramic technology was a significant innovation into these cultures; (2) ceramics of all kinds are major time markers; (3) the ceramic-using cultures have been studied the most extensively in Florida and thus are better defined; and (4) after the introduction of pottery, certain aspects of society seem to intensify even though the hunter-gatherer-fisher way of life persisted in most of Florida.

The Ceramic period in Florida begins about 4000+ B.P. It is possible to divide this period into three phases as has been done with the Paleoindian and Archaic periods: (1) Early or Orange, dating from ca. 4000 to 3000 B.P. (2000–1000 B.C.); (2) Middle or Transitional, dating from ca. 3000 to 2500 B.P. (1000–500 B.C.); (3) Late or Regional, dating from ca. 2500 B.P. to historic contact (500 B.C.–A.D. 1500). This classification is not purely arbitrary; a great deal of effort has been expended to identify ceramic sequences in Florida. The time frames for the phases, however, remain somewhat flexible because major changes did not occur simultaneously in all areas or because precise documentation is not always available. It is also possible to define a fourth phase of the ceramic industry that is introduced during and influenced by historic contact. This phase will be discussed later in the Historic period section.

Early Ceramic

It is probably true that no radical changes in subsistence occur when pottery first appears in the archaeological record. But cultural traits besides pottery seem to make an appearance at this time, although some of these may have been introduced during the Late Archaic. Nevertheless, the constellation of new attributes may support the belief held by some individuals that pottery was not locally developed.

In the late nineteenth and early twentieth centuries, no one questioned that contact between Florida Indians and cultures to the south had taken place for a long time. The presumption of such connections did not come from archaeological evidence as much as from early historic literature; for example, the Solís de Merás account of Pedro Menéndez de Avilés's experiences in Florida. Eventually, the historic accounts citing specific incidences of communication between Florida Indians and those to the south were dismissed by many individuals as being erroneous or too recent to be indicative of long-term relationships. Skepticism about contact grew as the twentieth century progressed. Today opinion is divided, with some people saying that similarities are due to the "law of limited possibilities" or the "psychic unity of man," and others declaring that there are too many duplicate traits, perhaps beginning in the Late Archaic, to discount a contact situation.

The most obvious item for comparison from the archaeological record is fiber-tempered ceramics. In fact, if it were not for the parallelism noted in ceramics between northern South America and the coasts of Georgia and Florida, other, perhaps older, evidence may have gone unobserved. Major questions to consider are: Is it only a coincidence that the earliest ceramics in North America appear first on the east coast of Georgia and Florida, that they are fiber-tempered, and that some of the designs on the pottery are similar to those from northern South America? The Indians may desperately have needed a technology to process the huge quantities of shells they were harvesting by 6000 B.P. **Clay balls**, found at many Late Archaic sites (part of the Elliott's Point complex in Florida), may have served as boiling "stones" to heat foods in containers that could not be set directly on a hearth. Also, fired clay lumps may have served as a substitute for hearth stones in areas where suitable stones were not available. These comments may not be the answer to why ceramic technology developed indigenously or diffused along with other traits, but there is no question that it was an instant success once it arrived.

For at least 100 years, Orange Series ceramics have been recognized as the earliest manifestation of the ceramic industry in Florida. The name comes from a site on the St. Johns River in Orange County, but the ceramics of this period are referred to just as frequently as "fiber-tempered" because fibers (probably Spanish moss or something similar) were added as temper to the clay before it was fired. This pottery is very distinctive (fig. 1.26) because of the rough surface caused by the burned-out plant fibers, although in some cases the surfaces were smoothed. The clay was hand molded, rather than coiled, to shape the pots, which were usually rectangular with flat bases. As mentioned earlier, no woven materials have survived from this period in Florida, but from this time onward, numerous weaving patterns have been identified from pot bottoms (fig. 1.27). Where a stratigraphic sequence exists, fiber-tempered ware always underlies more recent ceramic types. Its earliest occurrence is on the coast of Georgia and in the northern St. Johns River region in Florida. Orange Plain sherds recovered from a water-saturated deposit at Lake Monroe (8Vo2601) were dated as early as 4100 B.P.

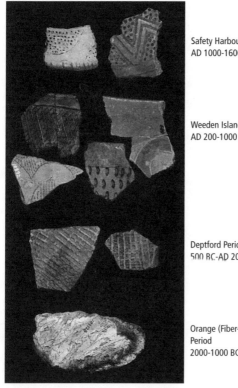

Safety Harbour period
AD 1000-1600

Weeden Island Period
AD 200-1000

Deptford Period
500 BC-AD 200

Orange (Fiber-Tempered)
Period
2000-1000 BC

1.26. Pottery sherds from several time periods, showing various design motifs. Color differences result from firing methods and temperatures, tempering materials, composition of clays, and postdepositional alteration. (Courtesy of Ann S. Cordell.)

1.27. Weaving patterns from pot bottoms. (Casts courtesy of Grant Groves.)

Orange Plain is considered the earliest pottery in Florida and Georgia, with Orange Incised and Tick Island Incised following somewhat later (fig. 1.28). This observation is undoubtedly correct because some of the incised designs that occur on Orange period sherds and on bone artifacts are carried over to the Middle or Transitional phase (fig. 1.29). Orange period ceramics are found around nearly the entire perimeter of Florida as well as near the St. Johns River and its tributaries such as the Ocklawaha and the Wekiva, and in the area of the Indian River, Lake Okeechobee, the Everglades, etc. They are also found sparingly at some Central Florida inland sites such as Bolen Bluff. Orange pottery may not be as early in South Florida or the Gulf Coast as it is in Northeast Florida. In some places, pottery dates only from the Middle Ceramic or Transitional phase.

To my knowledge the appearance about this time of corner-notched or basally notched spearheads has not been recognized as possibly having been stimulated by an external source. Yet, at a time when stone tool manufacture seems to have declined in Florida, it is strange that beautifully made stone points show up that deviate significantly from those of previous time periods. Except for stylistic changes, the differences are not too obvious in photographs, but if one examines these specimens, it is apparent that they are usually made of high-quality flint material (very often heat-altered silicified

1.28. Orange period sherds with designs from Groves Orange Midden site.

0   1   2
cm

A

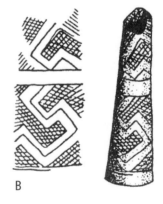

B

1.29 (a) Design on a pottery sherd from the Tick Island site, Volusia County, Florida, compared to (b) design on a bone artifact from the Bilbo site, Georgia.

coral), the workmanship is superior, and the resulting forms are usually smaller and more delicate than Archaic types (fig. 1.30). While they are sometimes found in Late Archaic strata (although this association is not always clear), they have definitely been recovered at sites containing fiber-tempered pottery.

Less conspicuous or not as thoroughly studied as ceramics is the increase about 5,000 years ago in marine shell technology, the use of coastal resources, an elaboration of designs on some bone artifacts and, perhaps, changing burial patterns.

An intriguing additional bit of evidence supporting external influences is the linguistic link postulated between the Timucuan Indians of Northeast Florida and the Warao language of the Orinoco Delta in South America.

> The basic phonological, morphemic, syntactic, and semiological structures and process of Timucua show well over 75 percent agreement with twentieth-century Warao. Lexically, seventeenth-century Timucua shares 55 percent cognates with Warao. There is also a lexical stratum in both modern Warao and seventeenth-century Timucua—approximately 25 percent in Timucua—which seems assignable to a Proto-Arawak (perhaps Proto-Maipuré) level. In addition, 10 percent of the Timucua vocabulary is derivable from Proto-Gulf sources, another 5 percent from a later specifically Proto-Muskhogean level, and the remaining 5 percent from Late Muskhogean. (Granberry 1971)

Muskhogean is the language group to which most of the Indians in the southeastern United States belonged (Creeks, Choctaws, Chickasaws, etc.). If Granberry's interpretation is correct, the Indians of Northeast Florida shared more language similarities with people from northern South America than

1.30. Basally and corner-notched stone points of the Early Ceramic period. (From Purdy 1981.)

0   2   4
cm

they did with their geographically closer neighbors. Granberry's evidence also suggests that these linguistic connections may be ancient in that a pre-Timucua group split from the proto-Waroid about 3000–2000 B.C. and began to migrate to the Florida peninsula. Such voyages were possible. There is archaeological and early historic documentation for the existence of large canoes capable of traveling with many occupants and much cargo across vast expanses of water.

The term **formative** is often used to refer to this cultural stage. It was initiated for areas, particularly Middle and South America, when plant cultivation became important. It is probably misleading, therefore, to use "formative" where plant cultivation was not practiced or has not been well documented (see below and chapter 3 for a discussion of the evidence for plant cultivation in Florida). It may be appropriate to use the term *formative* to emphasize that important changes were occurring.

Bullen (1972) summarized his interpretations of the Orange period. He divided the period into five subphases. Orange 1, the oldest, lasted for several hundred years and consisted of nothing but plain fiber-tempered sherds. Orange 2 is identifed by Orange Incised and Tick Island Incised pottery that overlie Orange Plain at sites where stratigraphic sequences exist. Orange 3 phase ceramics contain different designs and are more recent. Orange 4 fiber-tempered sherds have less elaborate decoration and tend to show a continuity into the Transitional period because of similarity in designs. Bullen is somewhat uncertain if Orange 5 belongs in the Orange or Transitional period because it includes a mix of types from both traditions that may have coexisted for a short time before fiber-tempering disappears.

I believe the chronology presented by Bullen for the Early Ceramic period is basically correct. The problem is that some of his conclusions are based on evidence from a single site or a single date, and the chronologies of his subphases tend to overlap so that it is not always clear if the differences are chronological or regional. The dates themselves may not be too accurate either, since many of them came from marine shell, which is not usually as desirable for dating purposes as other materials, and since some of the evaluations were made long ago, before refinements were made in radiocarbon dating. One specimen had even been treated with a preservative. Still, Bullen has demonstrated that fiber-**tempered** pottery occurs from the northern Gulf Coast of Florida at least as far south as Key Marco and on the east coast from the Florida border to the South Indian Fields site. The entire period lasted for approximately 1,000 years.

1.31. Steatite bead from Groves Orange Midden (8VO2601), Volusia County, Florida. Steatite is not native to Florida.

Bullen makes an important statement when he points out that the close of the Orange period occurred at approximately the same time as the beginning of the Woodland period and the first appearance of pottery in northern states around 1000 B.C. (Bullen 1959)—1,000 years after its arrival in Florida. This northern pottery usually was not fiber-tempered. In this regard, Bullen (1959) says that steatite vessels were manufactured in the North after pottery was being produced in Florida and that a knowledge of the ceramic industry may have stimulated the manufacture of steatite bowls even though other kinds of artifacts made of steatite, such as net weights, were present in archaeological sites at least by Archaic times (fig. 1.31). He offers as supporting evidence the fact that steatite vessel fragments are not found in Florida earlier than the Orange period and that they sometimes exhibit similar decoration. It should be noted that steatite is always rare in Florida and is usually fragmentary.

Middle Ceramic

During this time, also called Transitional, ceramics become progressively less fiber-tempered and incorporate tempering of sand, sponge spicules (often called temperless pottery), and occasionally sherd fragments. The entire phase is sometimes referred to as "semi-fiber-tempered" or "Norwood" in certain parts of Florida. These different tempering agents tend to become fairly regional through time as compared to the statewide homogeneity of fiber-tempered ware during the Early Ceramic. Some coiled, rather than hand-molded, vessels occur, and coiling becomes the standard by the Late Ceramic phase. Pottery from this time, especially in the St. Johns River region and vicinity, is still decorated to a certain extent. New vessel shapes and styles appear and some of these may have been introduced from outside Florida.

While pottery is the component of material culture that has been examined the most intently, it is not the most important feature of the Middle Ceramic phase. As pointed out earlier, Florida was never completely devoid of influences from other areas; for example, the 10,000-year-old bolas from the Paleoindian period were made of nonlocal stone. As cultures became more complex throughout the Southeast, Florida transmitted to and received ideas from other regions. Parts of the Southeast, especially along the Mississippi River and other large river systems, may have been influenced in turn by contact with Middle American cultures such as the Olmec. Selected traits of this contact seem to have filtered into Florida along the Gulf coast. Consequently, the Gulf Coast of Florida becomes the area where the most profound changes begin to take place, and the St. Johns region of East Florida, formerly the center of much innovation, is insulated and isolated from many of these developments.

But what is the real nature of developments around 1000–500 B.C.? Based on knowledge of early Mid-Eastern cultures in the Old World, it is usually assumed that people do not adopt pottery technology until plants and animals are domesticated and sedentary village life begins. When people are nomadic, it is logical that they would not want to be burdened by heavy and easily breakable ceramic pots. Following this scenario, it was concluded that when people began to use pottery in Florida they also had agriculture. But the scenario has no script; that is, there is no archaeological evidence for plant cultivation in Florida during the Early and Middle Ceramic phases. Throughout the entire southeastern United States, there is no indication that cultivated plants played a major role in survival at this time. In peninsular Florida, there are no archaeological finds to support the belief that plant cultivation *ever* existed prehistorically. The conclusion that corn and other plants were being raised is based on the accounts of Narváez or de Soto that describe their expeditions through Florida in the early 1500s. Based on evidence accumulated so far, it appears that the introduction and acceptance of the ceramic industry resulted from sedentism but not from the cultivation of crops. The harvest from aquatic resources was evidently fertile enough to give birth to sedentism.

Bottle gourds (*Lagenaria siceraria*) and ornamental gourds (*Cucurbita pepo*) have been recovered at archaeological sites. They may have been present as early as the Paleoindian period. These plants are usually considered **culti- gens,** but it is possible they occurred naturally. They were probably used for containers rather than food.

The increasing cultural complexity that is observed during the Transitional phase probably can be attributed to larger and more concentrated populations, sedentary villages near aquatic resources, and influences resulting from trade networks. It is a fact that aquatic resources can support fairly large sedentary populations, such as that on the Northwest coast of North America, with well-developed social hierarchies, including hereditary positions and specialists. A society that becomes differentiated into divisions of labor based on attributes other than merely sex and age usually can be recognized from the archaeological record. For example, important people might be found buried with elaborate grave goods or in special areas; settlements might contain evidence of large structures (either the chief's house or a ceremonial center); pottery designs and shapes might become more standardized and regionalized when specialists produce it as compared to when it was manufactured by each family; and existing technologies (such as bone and shell) become elaborated with more ornaments added to the typically manufactured utilitarian objects. The increase in ornamentation may be an indication of high social status of some individuals and of more free time for certain specialists to devote to making decorative items. There is little concrete evidence in Florida to demonstrate that the above statements are fact. One thing is certain, however: most of the important action in Florida was taking place where aquatic species could be harvested and in places that were on the main path of diffusion.

The Transitional phase lasted for approximately 500 years. The reader is reminded that this is a very long time. While some changes are apparent from the archaeological record, they probably occurred so gradually that the people who were modifying their culture hardly recognized that they were taking place.

Late Ceramic

In previous sections, the Paleoindian, Archaic, and Early and Middle Ceramic periods were defined primarily using temporal differences and the occurrence of a few diagnostic artifacts. Evidence of these early homogeneous populations is found throughout the state, even though it is recognized that some areas were more heavily populated than others. A new dimension, regionalism, is added with the onset of the Late Ceramic phase.

The various archaeological regions established within the state beginning with the Late Ceramic phase are frequently referred to as **culture areas** (fig. 1.32). The Culture Area Concept was put forward in the early twentieth cen-

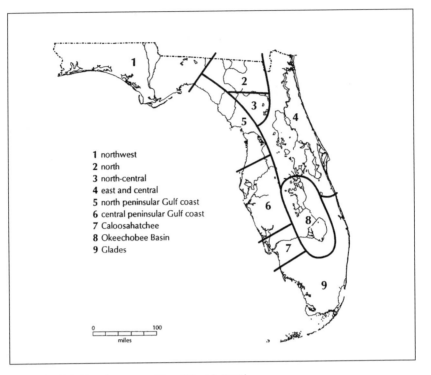

1 northwest
2 north
3 north-central
4 east and central
5 north peninsular Gulf coast
6 central peninsular Gulf coast
7 Caloosahatchee
8 Okeechobee Basin
9 Glades

0   100
miles

1.32. Map of Florida culture areas. (From Milanich 1994.)

tury in an effort to divide the Indian groups of America into meaningful categories so they could be studied analytically. The traits that were used to establish culture areas included subsistence, ceremonialism, language, artifacts, physical type, geographic contiguity, environment, and so on. As an example, the Northwest Pacific Coast of North America was delineated as a culture area because the Indians were maritime peoples who practiced no agriculture, used no pottery, and shared similar social, ceremonial, and woodworking traditions. While these traits become somewhat indistinct on the peripheries of the culture area, they nevertheless tend to cluster in ways that separate the Northwest Coast from that of California to the south, the Plateau to the east, and the Arctic to the north.

There were language affinities also, but they played little part in the formation of the Northwest Coast culture area because various linguistic groups were present within the area and linguistic ties existed with people from entirely different culture areas. The Navaho and Apache of Arizona and New Mexico, for instance, are linguistically and physically related to several Northwest Coast groups. A major flaw with the Culture Area Concept is that it makes little allowance for time depths and the possibility that some areas may have contracted or expanded through time. It appears that environment, subsistence, ceremonialism, certain artifacts, and geographic contiguity are the attributes that are the most important in establishing culture areas.

Can these criteria be applied to the creation of culture areas in Florida? Despite claims for the cultivation of crops among the Indians of peninsular Florida, there is virtually no substantial evidence that beans, corn, or squash were grown prehistorically. No rivers with extensive alluvial plains exist in peninsular Florida to make planting easier and more attractive. The Indians of Northwest Florida (the Panhandle) apparently grew some corn by A.D. 900, but this occurred 1,400 years after the Late Ceramic phase began. Aquatic resources formed the subsistence base throughout most of the state, but exploitation strategies must have differed because of the change from a temperate climate in northern Florida to a subtropical climate in the south. Cultural contrasts should be detectable also between a coastal way of life, a riverine way of life, or a way of life dependent upon resources of inland lakes or cultivation of crops. Most of the tool kit, however, looks superficially much the same throughout the state except for differences in ceramic styles; shell, bone, and stone tools (where present) are quite similar everywhere. Ceremonial objects and decorations may vary but their regional significance is ill-defined. It is quite possible that art objects, especially those made of wood, may furnish a clearer definition of regional cultures than do utilitarian objects or environmental differences (fig. 1.33).

In contrast to the Northwest Pacific Coast culture area described above, linguistic groups did occupy distinct areas of Florida, at least during the Early Historic period. Partial vocabularies of three major languages have been recorded: the Calusa who occupied the southwestern Gulf Coast and may have included the Tequesta and Keys Indians as well as other groups; the Timucua, who lived in Northeast and North Central Florida and may have been linguistically related to the Tocobago in the Tampa area; and the Apalachee, located in the Florida Panhandle between the Apalachicola and the Aucilla Rivers. Linguistic relations are not known for the hunter-gatherer-fisher Ais and Jeaga, who occupied a portion of the southeastern Florida coast, and the already mentioned Tequesta, Keys, and Tocobago Indians.

The physical characteristics of Florida Indians, as determined from studies of skeletal remains recovered throughout the state, are fairly uniform, as are their pathologies, injuries, nutrition, and ages at death. These similarities in-

1.33. Wood carvings of animals. Compare (a) carving from the Thursby site on the St. Johns River near Hontoon Island (possibly an otter holding a fish), approximately A.D. 1200, to (b) carving from the Fort Center site (otter with a fish in its mouth), approximately A.D. 500 (Sears 1982). Both specimens are made from pine and both depict animals, but the art styles are very different.

clude shovel-shaped incisors, extreme tooth wear and abscessing, evidence of disease on skulls and postcranial bones, arthritis, syphilis, and congenital or developmental abnormalities such as head deformation. Based on studies of skeletal remains, the overall health of most Florida Indians was generally good, but keep in mind that only bones and teeth have survived to draw this conclusion; obviously, something was killing them that might be identified if other tissues had been preserved. In addition, the average age at death was not very old (probably less than 30 years), so that maladies sometimes manifest on skeletons of older adults had not yet developed prior to the time these people died.

There is little question that social structure became more complex in certain areas of Florida during the Late Ceramic phase. This complexity is apparent from settlement patterns, ceremonial structures, human skeletal remains, a few classes of artifacts, and ritual associated with burial practices. Many features, however, were merely frosting on the cake, and Florida Indians, for the most part, remained aquatically oriented throughout nearly all of the state's later prehistory. Information about actual lifeways tends to remain fairly speculative because concrete evidence is often lacking and interpretations are still based primarily on changes in the types of bowls people were making; i.e., the shapes, designs, and pastes of the ceramic industry (fig. 1.26). If ceramics were removed from the cultural inventory, it is doubtful that the archaeological record would furnish enough significant, detectable variations in the material or social culture of Florida Indians during the Late Ceramic phase to warrant creating separate culture areas. One should expect to see more complex development in areas such as the Gulf Coast, where resources were plentiful or where a great deal of cultural diffusion occurred. In other locations, such as the St. Johns River, resources were abundant but evidently the area was effectively isolated for hundreds of years from outside influences, or the inhabitants did not care to incorporate innovations into their social systems. The St. Johns River, like the Nile River in Africa, was a natural world tied together by moving water.

The long time span of the Late Ceramic or Regional phase has been divided into three subphases that date roughly 500 B.C.–A.D. 0, A.D. 0–1000, and A.D. 1000–1500. These subphases are more apparent in some regions of Florida than in others. Based on results of past field work and numerous reports of investigations, these subphases and regional expressions have been summarized and clarified.

500 B.C.–A.D. 0

Three broad regional adaptations are recognized for this subphase: Gulf Coast Deptford, St. Johns, and South Florida.

On the west coast of Florida, the Deptford people occupied salt marsh locations near tidal streams, introduced sand-tempered pottery that apparently originated in a similar ecologic zone on Georgia's Atlantic coast, and probably moved inland during certain times of the year to hunt deer and harvest hickory nuts. Several natural habitats were exploited along the Gulf Coast but the major subsistence items were fish, shellfish, and even sea mammals. Acorns were available from nearby hammocks and may have been another important source of food. Small populations would have had nearly unlimited resources. Some Deptford sites are believed to be underwater now because of sea level rise. Deptford pottery was paddle-stamped to compact coils. Simple, linear, check, and other stamped designs are present. Vessels were deep and cylindrical-shaped with rounded (conoidal) bottoms except for those with tetrapods or tripods, which had squared or flat bases (fig. 1.34). The presence of podal bases on some pots suggests a cultural connection with Woodland cultures (Adena/Hopewell) to the north. Deptford ceramics are found at inland sites and along the St. Johns River and its drainage but are not common.

1.34. Deptford period ceramic vessel with tetrapod base. (From Goodyear 1969; photo by Francis Bushnell.)

How can we account for the presence of a few Deptford sherds at sites outside of the core area other than to assume they were dropped and broken during seasonal rounds? If the Deptford style pots themselves were desired, it seems that they would be found in greater numbers and might even replace local types. Perhaps Deptford pots were used to transport trade goods across the state, comparable to the way amphorae (large vases), found at Mediterranean shipwreck sites, were used in the Old World. For example, spearheads made of high-quality chert material (often silicified coral) that outcrops in West, but not East, Florida are frequently found at sites along the St. Johns River. They may have been transported by canoes in ceramic pots. Another possible explanation is that there may have been wife exchange from the Gulf Coast to locations outside the area. The brides may have brought Deptford-style pots with them, some of which may have been filled with "dowry" items. These are probably far-fetched speculations that should not be considered as fact, but they are presented in an effort to repeople the landscape and portray human social behavior not directly related to subsistence patterns.

Nonceramic artifacts are not very spectacular until Late Deptford times. A few shell, bone, and stone tools as well as shell beads have been recovered. Around 100 B.C.–A.D. 100, a growth in ceremonialism occurs in the Gulf Coast area. The famous Crystal River State Archaeological Site has provided the most complete record for the area of what is called the Yent ceremonial complex, which was probably introduced from Northwest Florida. Burial mounds contained various kinds of copper artifacts and ornaments, plummets and gorgets made of local and non-Florida raw materials, cut carnivore jaws, special kinds of pottery (some with **kill holes**) not found in the village area, and conch shell drinking cups, indicating that the **black drink** (*Ilex vomitoria*) was consumed. The Yent complex probably also included an elite class of people who had hereditary privileges, charnel houses, and religious specialists to carry out sacred functions. This complex seems to have been the start of ceremonial activities that continued until the Historic period.

In the eastern part of the state, from the Georgia-Florida border in the north to at least the Indian River area, from about 500 B.C. to A.D. 100, the St. Johns I people produced mostly plain pottery bowls. This ceramic type, initiated in the Transitional period, is often called chalky wear because it contains few sand grains or fibers; its smoothness comes from the presence of sponge spicules that serve as temper. The predominant technique to manufacture bowls is coiling. Sand burial mounds also occur for the first time, replacing interment directly in shell middens. The presence of bundled buri-

1.35. Charnel house. (Painting
by John White of Virginia
between 1585 and 1587,
engraving by De Bry.)

als suggests that charnel houses were still used to store bodies until the flesh
rotted away, after which the bones were disarticulated, bundled, and placed
in the mound (fig. 1.35). Red ochre (hematite) was sprinkled on the bones.
This custom has been documented for even earlier periods and in Europe
dates to Neanderthal times about 40,000 years ago. Various explanations have
been given for the use of red ochre with burials; these include the belief that
it makes the corpse appear healthy or that, because hematite may have some
curative benefits, the dead will return to life either in this world or in the
hereafter. Extended, flexed, or cremated remains are also present in the sand
mounds. Grave goods are rare and there is no indication that only special
people were buried in the mounds.

Why do so many different kinds of burials occur at these sites? In our cemeteries, burials tend to be very similar. A possible explanation might be that a

grand burial ceremony occurred only once a year or at infrequent intervals. At that time, all of the corpses stored in the charnel house would be prepared for final burial. Those that had died recently and still retained most of their flesh could not be disarticulated and bundled (**secondary burial** method) so they remained extended or flexed (**primary burial** method). It is difficult to explain cremation, however. By referring to **ethnographic** data gathered around the world, one discovers that in some areas interment varies depending upon how death occurred or upon an individual's status or position in society. Not only is the chief accorded special recognition but also the shaman, the talented woodcarver, the great hunter, etc., and all differ. Slaves are often just dumped somewhere.

These sites occur along the St. Johns River and its tributaries and the Atlantic coast, where huge oyster middens attest to the fact that this mollusk was an important subsistence item. Freshwater aquatic species dominate in the shell middens along the river. Most food items and artifacts remain much as they were during Orange and Transitional times.

Widespread occupation in South Florida seems to date from about 500 B.C., although there is evidence from Cutler, Little Salt Spring, Warm Mineral Springs, Bay West, Republic Groves, Santa Maria, Cheetum, Fort Center, and other sites that South Florida was inhabited during the Late Paleoindian, Middle and Late Archaic, and Transitional (semi-fiber-tempered ceramic) periods. Nevertheless, cultural changes in South Florida around 500 B.C. included the introduction of black earth middens, the construction of circular drainage ditches, plain sand-tempered pottery (also called Glades I), nonlocal materials such as mica, steatite, igneous rock, platform pipes, marine shell, and chert, although this latter material appears at earlier sites also. Primary and secondary burials contain few grave goods. Many types of animals were utilized. Practically nothing is known about plant remains from this time. South Florida, according to some authors, was a cultural cul-de-sac (Willey 1949a). It may have received influences from Middle and South America, and it interacted with cultures on the Gulf Coast and along the St. Johns River. There is also strong evidence that it may have affected and been affected by Hopewellian cultures as far away as the Ohio Valley.

A.D. 0–1000

On the west and northwest coast of Florida, the Swift Creek and Weeden Island cultures replace Deptford around A.D. 0–100+. An amazing amount of literature exists about the ceramics (and their origins) of this time as well as more limited information about lifestyles. **Relative dates** for various Weeden Island subphases were proposed early in the twentieth century, and ceramic sequences were well established by the 1940s. There has been refinement of these subphases in more recent years.

The Deptford, Swift Creek, and Weeden Island cultural traditions fall within the time periods of Early to Middle Woodland (also called Adena and Hopewell) in the eastern United States that are most conspicuous in the Ohio Valley and nearby vicinities. There was a well-organized trade network, called by archaeologists the *interaction sphere*, whereby material objects from one area traveled to other locations. For example, marine conch shells from Florida

1.36. Effigy vessel, Weeden Island period, Washington County, Florida. (Courtesy of the National Museum of the American Indian, Smithsonian Institution, New York.)

have been found outside of their natural Gulf Coast habitat, and copper, probably from the Great Lakes, has been recovered in Florida. Some authors propose that the primary function of the interaction sphere was economic while others believe it was religious or political. It may have been a combination of all of these, and more, with certain individuals, groups, or centers becoming prestigious, powerful, and awesome depending upon their ability to control desired resources. Ideas must have flowed also but are not visible archaeologically. The material results of some of the ideas can be identified, such as an emphasis on burial mound ceremonialism and new pottery designs. Fig. 1.36 illustrates one example of the multitude of shapes and designs modeled from clays into three-dimensional representations.

Burials were placed in mounds used specifically for the dead. In some mounds there is evidence that original interments were made at ground level and later became the center of a mound that grew as dirt or sand and more burials were added. Pottery caches were sometimes placed on the east side of the mound. The Weeden Island site at Tampa Bay supplied the name to this cultural expression dating from approximately A.D. 0 to 1000. Subsequent research, however, has shown that the most elaborate components of this time are found in North Florida and Georgia. Variations have also been noted based on time, geographic location, and cultural antecedents. Researchers are generally in agreement that the origin of some Weeden Island traits came from the Kolomoki site in Georgia. But Willey (1985) makes a plea for cultural diffusion from afar, saying, "I hope you will not altogether forget the possibility of more remote and exotic contacts. It seems to me highly likely that the Middle Woodland (Hopewell and Weeden Island) ... ceramic flamboyance of the Florida Gulf Coast must have something to do with its relative proximity to Mesoamerica." These connections wait to be demonstrated.

The variations noted at Weeden Island sites have been subdivided into Weeden Island I-V depending upon time and space factors. Around A.D. 100–300, just prior to Weeden Island and overlapping with Deptford, Swift Creek Complicated Stamped pottery is introduced from Woodland cultures to the north. The stamping is achieved by using a carved wooden paddle. It is largely a distinct ceramic style that replaces Deptford in some locations and is recovered around the Gulf Coast from west of Pensacola as far south as Crystal River. At the same time, some influences called Santa Rosa arrive from west of Florida's Panhandle. Weeden Island I is noted for its ornately decorated ceramics with animal effigies and triangular cutouts. During Weeden Island II–III, complicated stamped pottery decreases and is supplanted by Wakulla

Check Stamped, which prevails until Weeden Island V, when it is replaced by Safety Harbor and Fort Walton period pottery.

The McKeithen site in Columbia County is a classic Weeden Island site that has attributes similar to those at the Kolomoki site in Georgia. It dates from A.D. 200 to 700; has multiple mounds; effigy vessels; pottery caches; and evidence of the use of charnel houses, the black drink ceremony, and red ochre. It grew out of Yent and Green Point ritual traditions. Weeden Island continued even when Hopewell cultures and the interaction sphere declined around A.D. 400.

Cades Pond is a Weeden Island–related cultural expression. Cades Pond sites occur from the Santa Fe River on the north to Orange Lake on the south and in eastern Alachua and western Putnam and Clay Counties. Villages were located on high ground next to lakes or swamps and were probably occupied most of the year. Subsistence items included fish, freshwater shellfish, turtles, snakes, birds, deer, and hickory nuts. Storage pits have been identified at some sites. The primary features that connect Cades Pond to Weeden Island are the presence of burial and platform mounds. The mounds contain exotic materials such as plummets made of imported stone, copper beads, marine shells, and bones of shark, sea turtles, and mullet. The sites date from A.D. 100 to 400 and are similar to Crystal River and Fort Center, with separate sacred/secular areas and evidence of the use of charnel houses. Cades Pond sites also contain St. Johns and Dunns Creek Red ceramics (see below), indicating that there was considerable interaction with people to the east.

The Manasota culture of the peninsular Gulf Coast dates within the time frame of Weeden Island and shares a few of its attributes. It has been distinguished from cultures to the north of Tampa Bay and south of Charlotte Harbor based primarily on ceramic differences.

In East Florida, along the St. Johns River and adjacent coastal areas, some influences arrive from West and Northwest Florida. Copper objects, green stone celts, jasper beads, and clay elbow pipes have been found in a few locations, indicating that this region was not totally isolated. Shell, bone, and stone tools and ornaments apparently do not change very much from earlier times, and the basic way of life from A.D. 0 to 1000 probably remained essentially as before. Burials were placed in sand mounds and consisted of both primary and secondary interments. The primary ceramic type is St. Johns Plain. Some pottery, called Dunns Creek Red, had a red slip applied and is usually found in burials. Sites like Tick Island could have provided clues to temporal

1.37. Comparison of Florida stone points from Paleoindian to Late Ceramic periods.

0   2   4
cm

variations, but they were not excavated in ways that could furnish this information.

Archaeological sites that have been excavated systematically are usually examined intensively rather than extensively. Minute information about diet, climate, and typical material items may be identified but large quantities of artifacts, other than pottery sherds, usually are not recovered. Thus it is not likely that many exotic specimens will be found or that any class of objects will be available in numbers sufficient for statistical analysis that would reveal significant changes through time. At Hontoon Island, a garbage midden, the overwhelming ceramics (about 100,000 sherds) recovered within this A.D. 0–1000 time range were St. Johns Plain with a chalky paste. Marine shell and bone tools resembled those of former times. Most of the diagnostic chert artifacts were Pinellas points (fig. 1.37). Pottery clays and animal bones were available locally; marine shell and chert had to be imported, but not from very far away. The only other nonlocal material recovered from the garbage midden at Hontoon Island from A.D. 0 to 1000 was a few fragments of green stone. The midden contained convincing evidence of an aquatic diet consisting primarily of fish, shellfish, and turtles. If a more elaborate way of life existed, it was probably reserved for ritual associated with burials. Unfortunately, burial mounds have been destroyed in order to retrieve items considered valuable by nineteenth-century archaeologists and twentieth-century pothunters.

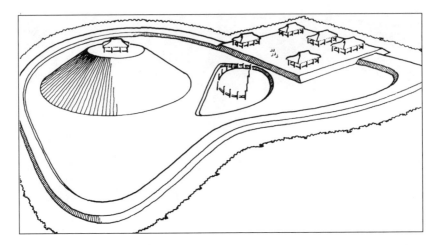

1.38. Stylized illustration of ceremonial area at the Fort Center site. (From Morgan 1980; Purdy 1991.)

There are several spectacular sites in South Florida that date within the A.D. 0–1000 time span. Belle Glade, Key Marco, and Fort Center have been excavated more or less systematically. The most thorough examination of a site and interpretation of a cultural complex and its temporal placement in South Florida comes from Sears's (1982) work at Fort Center. Portions of the site existed by 450 B.C. and eventually included middens, house mounds, earthworks, ceremonial mounds, and a charnel pond.

About A.D. 200, the inhabitants at Fort Center constructed a special area to prepare and bury their dead. This consisted of a low mound upon which was probably built a charnel house, a special activity area that may have served also as residences for specialists and their families, and an artificially dug pond with a platform where bundled burials were placed (the charnel pond). The mounds and the pond functioned as an integrated ceremonial area and the entire complex was separated from the rest of the village by a low sand embankment (fig. 1.38). Sometime around A.D. 500, the platform burned and collapsed into the pond carrying with it approximately 300 bundled burials and between 100 and 150 carvings or fragments of carvings thought to represent a total of 69 complete specimens (fig. 1.39). Many of these carvings had supported or decorated the platform; others may have accompanied the dead as grave goods. After the platform collapsed, 150 of the burials were retrieved from the pond, interred on top of one of the mounds, and then covered with white sand. The other 150 remained in the pond. The Fort Center site contin-

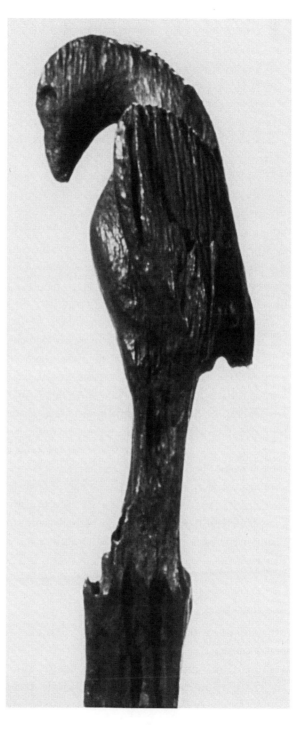

1.39. Wood carving of eagle from the Fort Center site. (Courtesy of Roy C. Craven, Jr.)

ued to be occupied after this catastrophe but the ceremonial complex of the site declined.

A situation at the Fort Center site that has sparked tremendous controversy and discussion is the presence of corn pollen in the ceremonial area. Sears (1982) interpreted the presence of corn pollen and other traits at the site as evidence that there was contact with South America and with Hopewellian cultures to the north. Sears's conclusion is supported by the recovery at Fort Center of exotic artifacts, including fragments of 74 pottery pipes that are nearly identical to those from Hopewell sites. Skepticism about the role of corn in stimulating the construction of the complex Fort Center site stems from the fact that (1) there is no other site in Florida where corn remains have been found at such an early date as period II at Fort Center, (2) there is no evidence that corn was important anywhere in the eastern United States around A.D. 200, and (3) a study of pollen remains in 21 human **coprolites** from the site revealed a variety of wild plants suggesting a random selection from the local habitats with minimal dietary dependence on any particular plant. No corn pollen was found in these 21 coprolites. Macrobotanical remains, such as corn cobs, were not preserved at the Fort Center site.

No radiocarbon dates exist for the Belle Glade site located on the southeastern shore of Lake Okeechobee, but the site shares many traits with Fort Center, including art styles executed on wooden carvings. In turn, the wooden artifacts can be linked with similar specimens from Key Marco, which has been dated to essentially the same time period as Fort Center. A number of other large sites, known as Big Circle Mounds, occur in South Florida, but these have not been examined carefully; consequently, very little can be said about their function, temporal placement, or relationship to other sites in the area and afar. Like Fort Center, they were probably constructed over a time span of several hundred years and partially within the A.D. 0–1000 period being discussed. If the Big Circle Mounds were examined more thoroughly, they might produce remains of corn in support of Sears's finds at Fort Center.

A.D. 1000–1500

Mississippian is the name given to the cultures of the southeastern United States during this time span. In Florida these cultures are known as Fort Walton in the Panhandle region, Safety Harbor around Tampa Bay, St. Johns IIa-b in East Florida, and Glades IIb and Glades IIIa-b in South Florida (most people do not consider Glades cultures as "Mississippian" in the Fort Walton

1.40. Copper breast plate from the Lake Jackson site. (Courtesy of Roy C. Craven, Jr.)

sense). The attributes usually associated with the Mississippian period include corn agriculture or horticulture; flat-topped temple mounds; and a ceremonial complex previously known as the Buzzard Cult or the Southern Cult, in which a number of motifs are executed on various material items, particularly ceramics made specially for burials of elite individuals. A few breast plates of copper have been recovered also in association with chiefly burials (fig. 1.40). The Pinellas point becomes the most common chipped stone implement. This small triangular stone point resembles those recovered from sites of this age throughout the Southeast and is thought to signal the adoption of the use of the bow and arrow. The bow and arrow was first in use 19,000 years ago in North Africa. It is believed that this technologically superior weapon was invented only once and that it eventually diffused throughout most of the world. If this conclusion is correct, it took from 19,000 B.P. to nearly A.D. 1000 to enter the southeastern United States. It never reached isolated groups such as the Australian Aborigines.

Impressive temple mounds in Florida include those at Fort Walton Beach and Lake Jackson near Tallahassee. Similar kinds of structures are found in the Tampa Bay area, further south on the Gulf Coast (for example, at Pineland and Mound Key), and in East Florida along the St. Johns River at the Mount Royal, Shields, and Thursby sites. These areas were occupied during the Early Historic period by the Apalachee, Tocobaga, Calusa, and Timucuan Indians, respectively. The temple mounds were probably constructed by the immediate ancestors of these historically described people, although numerous large temple mounds seem to have Weeden Island components. Artifacts other than exotic ceramics and copper breastplates remain quite similar to styles that were in use previously. A.D. 1000 marks the beginning of check-stamped pottery along the St. Johns River and surrounding areas (fig. 1.41).

The temple mounds usually contained a ramp that led to a plaza area. It is believed that only important people are buried in the temple mounds and that when a chief died the structure that was built for his residential or ceremonial use was destroyed. This individual was buried in the mound and that portion of the mound was covered over and another structure for the new chief was built on top of it. Some of these mounds contain numerous episodes of building and rebuilding. Because of the nature of Florida's soils and environment, very little physical evidence of those structures remains, although at some sites large pieces of wood, presumably used as house posts, have survived. The ceramics found in the temple mounds differ from the undecorated everyday village pottery, indicating a difference between secular and sacred use.

Much of the way of life portrayed for the people of the Mississippian period is based on historic accounts of Indian groups as they existed when first encountered by Europeans. One famous group was the Natchez Indians, who lived along the Mississippi River and were described vividly by DuPratz (Swanton 1946). Another account is that of Juan Ortiz, a member of Narváez's expedition of 1528, who was held captive by the Tocobaga around Tampa Bay until rescued by de Soto in 1539. There is probably a great deal of support for the belief that chiefdoms did exist, that these were not egalitarian societies (that is, there were social hierarchies and probably inheritance of important

1.41. St. Johns Check Stamped sherds from Hontoon Island.

positions), and that there was maize or corn agriculture in some locations. The red clay soils around Tallahassee were ideal for agriculture. However, in peninsular Florida around Tampa Bay where the Tocobaga resided, among the Calusa, the Glades people, and along the St. Johns River, the attributes seen that are associated with the Mississippian period were probably used for rituals that took place at the temple mounds. In addition, these locations may have been **central places** where the action was. People may have come to these centers to trade, meet friends, acquire spouses, and relieve boredom. There is no concrete evidence in these areas for agriculture or horticulture. Most aboriginal Floridians continued a way of life dependent primarily upon aquatic resources. The Alachua Tradition people who lived in North Central Florida about this time may have planted some crops, although no crop remains have been found. They did not construct temple mounds or make elaborately incised pottery. The Alachua Tradition evidently came from the river valleys of the Georgia coastal plain.

Further support for the existence of nonegalitarian societies during the Mississippian period comes from the fact that the common people were buried in cemeteries, mounds, pits, or village debris, whereas elite individuals are buried in temple mounds along with exotic artifacts.

The top portion of most of the large mounds contains Early Historic period items, indicating that these structures were still in use when European contact occurred after A.D. 1500. There is a possibility that some European goods made their way into Florida prior to actual contact between Europeans and Indians. A brief **protohistoric** period may have occurred if Indians from the Caribbean or South America fled to Florida shortly after A.D. 1492 in an effort to escape Spanish atrocities.

HISTORIC PERIOD

The Historic period in the Americas is a story of the decline of the American Indian and a way of life that had been evolving for at least 10,000 years. In Florida, this decline began in A.D. 1513 with the arrival of Juan Ponce de León. Exploratory or slaving expeditions may have occurred prior to this time, but they have not been documented. These earlier contacts may explain why the Indians of Florida were hostile to Ponce de León and all other groups that came later. There are several bits of information that suggest that nonlocal Indians and/or Europeans knew of Florida before Ponce de León's voyage. These include (1) a map from about A.D. 1500 that shows an outline of part of the Florida peninsula, (2) a name given to Florida by the Indians of the Bahamas, and (3) a Spanish-speaking Indian encountered by Ponce de León. There are also the comments made in Fontaneda's account (True 1944) that Indians from Cuba "anciently" entered Florida looking for the River Jordan (fountain of youth) and settled among the Calusa.

The European ventures that had the greatest impact on Florida and other locations in the Southeast were: Juan Ponce de León in 1513 and 1521, Lucas Vasquez de Ayllon in 1521, Pánfilo de Narváez in 1528, Hernando de Soto in 1539, Tristán de Luna y Arrellano in 1559, Jean Ribault in 1563, Pedro Menéndez de Avilés in 1565, and Juan Pardo in 1566. It is interesting to note that when de Luna's 1559 expedition traveled to some of the same villages described as lavish by de Soto 20 years earlier, they were either deserted or in a state of decline. Evidently de Soto set in motion a demographic collapse brought about by brutality and by the introduction of diseases for which the Indians had no natural immunity.

Almost from the beginning there were composite pictures drawn of Florida and the people who lived there. Each succeeding generation of scholars has refined the earlier descriptions as new documents are discovered in archives and translated. An excellent example of the way new information can be incorporated into an earlier publication is the revision of Buckingham Smith's 1854 translation of Hernando de Escalente Fontaneda's 17-year experience as a captive among the Florida Indians in the mid-1500s to be discussed below (True 1944).

A disturbing feature of some of the documents or illustrations pertaining to early expeditions is that chroniclers lifted whole passages describing or depicting scenes from South or Central America and attributed them to events experienced in Florida with no apology for plagiarism or misrepresentation. For example, Ponce de León used dogs against the Indians of Hispaniola, and their use in war led to the coining of a new word, *aperrear,* "to cast to the dogs." Gruesome tales of the use of dogs to track down Indians are to be found in narratives of de Soto's expedition. One account purporting to describe a dog owned by de Soto is identical to Herrera's story of a dog owned by Ponce de León.

Other examples are the drawings of Jacques le Moyne engraved by de Bry in 1591. They provide the best pictorial documentation of the Timucuan Indians and scenes from their daily life. Nevertheless, the natives look very much like European people depicted by artists of the time, and the pictures of artifacts are so stylized it is difficult in many cases to relate them to material items recovered from archaeological sites. While the written descriptions accompanying the pictures probably reflect the situation as it existed in Florida fairly well, the reader gets the impression that considerable embellishment occurred. The references to gold and silver sources is especially suspect and may have been included either because the author became confused with scenes from Central or South America or because he hoped to gain financial support to return to Florida. The writers and artists who visited the Americas themselves or depended for their portrayals on descriptions given by those who survived early explorations probably had limited personal experience or knowledge of the New World. They took liberties with the literature that was available and often incorporated scenes that look very much like European life of the fourteenth to sixteenth centuries (fig. 1.42). While the authenticity of le Moyne's drawings is questionable, they can be considered as accurate as written documents of the time that were often recounted from memory. Letters to the crown describing events shortly after they occurred probably furnish less questionable portrayals of life in Florida.

The Indians of Florida were taller than the French and Spanish intruders (fig. 1.43). The elite male members of society were tattooed extensively. They wore elaborate ornaments and painted deerskins. Spanish moss was used by

1.42. (a) LeMoyne drawing of a Timucuan Indian village (from Bennett 1968); (b) St. Mary's Wattle Chapel at Glastonbury. This famous site would have been known to LeMoyne. It was surrounded by legends and had been destroyed in 1539 (Michell 1983), only 25 years prior to the French settlement at Fort Caroline that led to LeMoyne's drawings and descriptions of the Florida Indians.

1.43. LeMoyne drawing showing a Timucuan chief taller than the Spaniards. (From Bennett 1968.)

women to make garments to "cover their nudity" (Bennett 1968: 78). Scenes from the le Moyne drawings show hunting, planting and harvesting crops, preparing food, shamanism, waging war, consuming the black drink, caring for the sick, punishing those who did not conform, villages, a chief's burial, and more.

Fontaneda's account of the Florida Indians (True 1944) is especially valuable because he lived among the Indians for 17 years, from the ages of 13 to 30. There seems to be some confusion as to the actual date of his capture, which followed the wreck of the ship that was transporting Fontaneda and his brother to Spain to be educated. His ordeal probably began sometime between 1545 and 1549, and his rescue took place in the early to middle 1560s. Some sources say he was rescued by Ribault and others say it was Menéndez. He evidently became an interpreter for Menéndez, but it is not clear if he stayed in Florida or returned from Spain after his rescue to perform this task. It would have helped if Fontaneda had related these details in his memoir, but their absence does not diminish the importance of his document, which was written in 1575, six years after he returned to Spain for good.

The memoir is the most compact description of Florida of that time. In it Fontaneda describes the geography and tells "of the Indians, their customs, habitat, language, clothing, and food. He describes animals, birds, fish, and plants. He relates contemporary events and makes recommendations for future Spanish policy" (True 1944). Fontaneda spoke at least four Indian languages. Though most of his captivity apparently was spent in the southern part of the Florida peninsula, particularly among the Calusa, many of his statements support the descriptions of the Timucuan Indians depicted by le Moyne. It is interesting to note that Fontaneda spent more of his first 30 years among the Indians than he did among his own people, yet in his document he expressed the opinion that "they never will be at peace, and less will they become Christians... I know what I say. If my counsel be not heeded, there will be trouble. Let the Indians be taken in hand gently, inviting them to peace; then putting them under deck, husbands and wives, together, sell them ... for money. In this way, there could be management of them, and their number become diminished" (True 1944). After 17 years of day-to-day relationships with the Florida Indians, it seems as if Fontaneda would have had some affection or compassion for them; instead he recommended their deportation and enslavement.

At least 30 other individuals who had spent many years among the Indians were rescued and returned home. Accounts of their experiences, if they exist, have not been discovered. Ships wrecked along the Florida coasts were plentiful, particularly in some areas. The ships were often laden with gold and silver being transported from South America back to Spain. Bad storms and hurricanes in the sixteenth and seventeenth centuries have been attributed partially to the "Little Ice Age," a climatic deterioration that occurred during this time. Since there was often too long a lag period between the loading of ships and their actual date of departure, many of them set sail during hurricane season and encountered the extremely hazardous weather conditions that caused the shipwrecks. These ships were plundered by the Indians and became the source of much of the precious metals, glass beads, and other European materials found in Florida. Fontaneda states that the natives took jewelry that was made by the Mexican Indians from the wrecks.

The Spanish began to establish Catholic missions in 1565, after they drove the French from Florida and founded St. Augustine as the earliest permanent settlement in North America. Since Fontaneda's (as well as Menéndez's) rec-

ommendation of deportation and enslavement of the Indians was not implemented, the missions served as a mechanism through which the Spanish could
strengthen their control over the natives. The missions functioned as distribution points in a network of trade and tribute of food, labor, and other
items. There was also a sincere desire on the part of the Jesuit and Franciscan
priests to convert the Indians to Catholicism. The first mission, known as
Nombre de Dios, was located at St. Augustine near the Indian village of Seloy.
Many other missions operated in Florida during the sixteenth and seventeenth
centuries. Gabriel Díaz Vara Calderón furnished a map showing the distribution of the missions in 1674–75.

The Indians of Florida attempted to maintain their social order and a measure of dignity despite the degradation of their way of life brought about by
the foreign intruders. Occasionally, the Indians revolted. Anthropologists
would call these revolts "revitalizaton movements" because they were efforts
to bring about a more meaningful existence for people in despair. They occurred among the Guale, Timucuans, Ais, and others. For example, after the
Timucuan uprising of 1656, the warriors claimed that "they sought only to
improve their low state and relieve the continuous abuses" (Lanning 1935:
206). Some **acculturation** took place in both directions. The Indians began
to rely on certain products such as European plants, animals, and metals; and
the Spanish, in order to survive, ate Indian foods and prepared their meals
using native dishes and cooking methods. Marriages between Spanish men
and Indian women also led to cultural exchanges and **assimilation** on a small
scale. Indian populations soon declined as a result of European- and African-
introduced diseases and from brutalities until, by the early eighteenth century, the original inhabitants had virtually disappeared from Florida, leaving
a void filled by the present-day Seminole Indians. The last of the original
Florida Indians are said to have left Florida with the Spanish when England
took over in 1763.

SUMMARY

By 35,000 years ago, Homo sapiens sapiens had evolved in the Old World
replacing previous hominid species, and the technology had been developed
permitting survival in nearly all ecological niches. It is possible, therefore,
that humans may have migrated to the Western Hemisphere by 25,000 to
30,000 years ago. However, this topic is hardly worth taking up at present
because there is no definite proof of such early human presence in the West-

ern Hemisphere. All sites that have been proposed have been evaluated carefully by competent archaeologists and so far all fall short of meeting the criteria necessary for acceptance. These criteria include: (1) rigid systematic excavations, (2) well-defined stratigraphy, (3) datable materials, and (4) recognizable artifact forms.

I have always believed that people were in the New World before 20,000 years ago, and I also believe that some of the proposed early sites are authentic despite the fact that results of investigations have not been conclusive. For example, at a chert quarry site in Marion County where I conducted excavations for several years, crude stone artifacts were recovered below Paleoindian period tools that probably date to about 10,000 years ago. The crude implements were typologically distinct from Paleoindian and were separated stratigraphically from them by a culturally sterile zone about 15–20 cm thick. No organic material was preserved that could be dated by radiocarbon analysis. Thus, I attempted to apply innovative techniques to determine the age of the crude stone artifacts. These methods included thermoluminescence and weathering experiments (see chapter 4). The preliminary results from these independently conducted studies yielded dates of 30,000–26,000 B.P. But unproven dating techniques applied to controversial materials need far greater testing before they will be accepted by the archaeological community. Here the story rests until further research is carried out. Earlier, however, I did mention two convincing dates for Florida of around 12,000 years ago, which might be considered proof of a pre-Clovis occupation.

As discussed at the beginning of this chapter, the presence of Clovis spearheads and butchered bones of now extinct animals furnish strong evidence for human habitation in Florida prior to the end of the last glacial period. Since the Clovis point has been tightly dated elsewhere at approximately 11,400–11,000 B.P. and is a very distinctive type, we can assume that those from Florida are contemporaneous. Unlike sites in the western United States, however, the Florida Clovis points are not in association with the extinct animals nor have they been recovered stratigraphically below typologically more recent materials. Elephant tusks have been found that were fashioned into tools, a few of which have zigzag lines that represent the earliest artistic efforts recovered in Florida. When found in rivers today, these tools are fossilized (turned to stone) and probably have been for thousands of years. Since ivory cannot be worked when it becomes fossilized, the native peoples of Florida must have been modifying it when it was green (fresh) or somewhat **seasoned**. As a result, there is no question about the age and authenticity of these ivory objects. Thus, we must conclude that humans and extinct Pleistocene (Ice Age) animals lived in Florida at the same time. So far, the deposits in which the extinct animals are imbedded have not contained evidence of human association; that is, no tools or human skeletal material. A possible exception are the Vero Beach and Melbourne bone beds. Human skeletal material was recovered from these bone beds in the early part of the twentieth century. Arguments have raged for decades about whether or not the human remains were contemporaneous with the extinct animals in the bone beds or were intrusive.

Aleš Hrdlička, an influential physical anthropologist of the time, was convinced that the cranial measurements were similar to those of modern-day Indians. He opposed those investigators who believed the skeletal material dated to the same period as the Ice Age animals. What Hrdlička really opposed were snap judgments about the antiquity of the human remains without the proof to back it up. Because he was such a prominent individual, his opinions and conclusions reigned for a very long time. Ironically, more recent evaluations of the human crania from the Vero Beach and Melbourne deposits suggest that Hrdlička's reconstructions were not accurate and that the crania actually may belong to a Paleoindian population.

Throughout all of North America there is virtually no human skeletal material that has been securely dated at 10,000 years or older. Human remains found at Warm Mineral Springs have been touted to be older than 10,000 years, but if one examines the 16 radiocarbon dates obtained from organic material recovered in association with these bones, it is clear that the dates range from 10,500 to 8700 B.P.; this suggests that some sort of sampling error or mixing occurred. Morris (in Purdy 1991:189–92) concluded that "Warm Mineral Springs Man" and the cranial material from the Vero Beach and Melbourne sites are doliocephalic (long-headed). He determined that there seems to be considerable variation in cranial measurements among Paleoindians, but that they can be distinguished from later Archaic populations. Since many of the human and animal remains still exist in various institutions, it is conceivable that certain analyses could be carried out on both animal and human bone to determine if they lived at the same time. Radiocarbon analysis would not be possible if the bones are fossilized.

From the Cutler site near Miami, the Warm Mineral Springs and Little Salt Spring sites near Sarasota, and the Page-Ladson site on the Aucilla River, human skeletal remains and/or cultural materials have been dated to about 9900–9600 B.P. and are associated with all modern fauna. Thus, the earliest *in situ* evidence for humans in Florida dates to this time period. It was then that Florida underwent very rapid climatic changes. Sea level rose, rivers flowed, passive ponds became springs, and low areas became lakes. In other words, previously scarce surface water became available.

The Paleoindian period is usually depicted as a nomadic, big game hunting way of life. A major new stage called the Archaic begins around 9000 B.P. and lasts until at least 4500 B.P. People became more sedentary as new resources became available and plentiful. There is an amazing increase in evidence of human occupation. For example, the Late Paleoindian stone points are fairly abundant in Florida, especially the Bolen point, which probably dates to the last part of the Paleoindian period. In fact, the Bolen point may signal the end of the nomadic way of life because it is found at some excavated terrestrial sites as well as in the rivers. The Harney Flats stone quarry site in Hillsborough County yielded Middle to Late Paleoindian stone tools, including Suwannee and Bolen points (Daniel and Wisenbaker 1987). This should be an indication that there were permanent residents in Florida at least by 9000+ B.P. On the other hand, most of the earlier Paleoindian types are rare or nonexistent from terrestrial sites, and there is little information to support the conclusion that people resided permanently in Florida at this time.

The beginning of the Archaic period in Florida has not been well documented. From stratified sites elsewhere in the southeastern United States, it appears that some of the Paleoindian tools are carried over into the Archaic, but that the stone spearheads change from the typical fishtail types of the Paleoindian period to the numerous stemmed varieties of the Archaic.

The Windover site is the only Early Archaic site in Florida that has been studied intensively. Since the dates for the Windover site range between approximately 8000 and 7000 B.P., it probably borders on the Middle Archaic. Chert artifacts are rare at Windover because the site is located away from chert outcrop regions. The few stone points found there resemble the Kirk Serrated, which is an Early Archaic stone point type in Florida. As mentioned earlier, Windover is a landmark site that contained a multitude of information that has not been recorded for any other site of this time period in Florida.

Around 7000–6000 B.P. during the Middle Archaic, many thousands of stone points were made and lost, only to be found again in the twentieth century. This is the time period that the major chert quarry sites were used most extensively. People were still seminomadic but within a restricted range of seasonal activities. This is also apparent from the great variety of stone points that are typical of the Middle Archaic indicating regional or tribal preferences. The incredible numbers of stone points that have been recovered leads one to conclude that Florida had large human populations, but no calculations have been attempted.

If only stone points are collected by amateurs, they are nice to look at and they furnish clues that people were hunting animals or other humans, but they are limited in what they can reveal about the total way of life of a society. Recall that the majority of the wetland cemeteries date to the Middle Archaic and contain the bones of hundreds of individuals plus diagnostic perishable and nonperishable artifacts in datable contexts. These sites date at about 6500–6000 B.P. They have provided all manner of information about burial practices, age and cause of death, food items, artifacts, and environment. Thus they have added tremendously to our storehouse of knowledge about Florida's prehistoric inhabitants. It is a mystery why the Indians changed this burial pattern.

By the Late Archaic, a different kind of cultural adaptation develops. Around 6000 B.P., Florida's flora, fauna, and hydrological conditions had adjusted to the changing climate. Numerous fish, shellfish, turtles, and plant species became abundant to the point that they could be predicted and relied upon as food staples, and the technology had been developed to exploit the resources efficiently. Aquatic species were the major dietary items along with deer and nuts. Our excavations at Lake Monroe demonstrated that people were using quantities of hickory nuts and acorns. Nut trees do not run away; the nuts are seasonally available; they provide protein, oil, calories, and other important nutrients; and they can be prepared in various ways or stored. No storage pits have been found in Florida that date to this time, but storage pits are common in other parts of the southeastern United States. We used hickory nut shells from the site at Lake Monroe to date the deposits. They ranged from 4100 B.P. at the top of the undisturbed sequence to 6200 B.P. for the lowest cultural deposit. An argument similar to that made for nuts can be proposed for turtles and tortoises. These slow-moving animals are fairly easy to catch under the right conditions and they return large amounts of edible flesh for very little effort. Archaeological evidence for their use is abundant.

The way of life that developed during the Late Archaic furnished the base upon which more complex societies evolved later on. This way of life probably was more secure than one dependent upon horticulture or animal husbandry. It should be cautioned, however, that people who rely on natural resources for their food supply and other needed items must limit their populations so as not to exceed the carrying capacity of the environment. They might be able to support a large population for a short time or a small population for a long time. Even with good management, some resources probably would be depleted. If too many items disappear, the group will most likely move to another location.

Most hunter-gatherer-fisher bands are no larger than 25 to 50 people. Since many of the plants and animals used by the aquatic-oriented Florida Indians were probably replenished fairly rapidly, there may have been short-term movements back and forth in the same general area over a long period of time. Unfortunately, we do not have a dating method that can provide a year-by-year record of activities from 6000 to 5000 B.P. Seasonal indicators may be reliable if, for example, plants and animals that are available only at certain times of the year turn up in the deposits. It would then be possible to say that a site was occupied during that time of the year, but it still would not be possible to conclude that the site was not utilized throughout the year because many of the items recovered would be obtainable year-round. The above discussion applied to the Florida situation is supported by Fontaneda's account. He mentions that there "are many towns of thirty or forty inhabitants each [around the Lake of Mayaimi (Lake Okeechobee)] and as many more places there are in which the people are not so numerous" (True 1944).

The Indians in Florida had been exploiting the aquatic resources for at least 1,500 years before ceramics were introduced. Fired clay balls, basally notched points, and marine shell tools and beads appear in the archaeological record prior to the appearance of pottery. Whether or not pottery was an indigenous development in North Florida and coastal Georgia is not known for sure. So far, no items exist that can be shown positively to have traveled to Florida from the Caribbean or Middle and South America. On the other hand, objects made from organic materials seldom survive and thus are not archaeologically visible. You may have noted that most perishable materials on exhibit in museums are ethnographic specimens that date to the Historic period. Prehistoric items are usually stone, shell, or ceramic. The Florida Indians were fairly sedentary by 4500–4100 B.P., when fiber-tempered (Orange period) pottery first appeared. These are the earliest ceramics in North America. The development of ceramic traditions through time and regionalism, defined primarily by ceramic styles, has already been discussed.

From the Late Archaic forward there seems to be an elaboration of the social life of the aquatically oriented peoples of Florida. What should the archaeological record reveal about societies that were becoming more complex and differentiated with regard to social structure and **division of labor**? There should be evidence of large populations with some kind of central control over people's actions with perhaps a warrior class to enforce order. Cultivation of crops such as corn should be present to support the increased population, or there should be evidence for the intensification of the use of natural resources. Important people would probably be buried in special areas with special grave goods. One would expect to find more ornamentation with recurring symbolism used as **badges of identity**. Village markers like large wooden carvings might appear (fig. 1.44).

What is known? What is not known? What is speculation rather than fact? There is evidence for central areas where ceremonies were performed and where people may have congregated to bring tribute, to relieve the boredom of a mundane existence, to procure spouses, and for numerous other reasons. We know that some people were buried in special areas, and there is increased ornamentation. But, from the archaeological record, there is very little concrete evidence in Florida of cultivation of corn, squash, and beans or of the cultivation or manipulation of other plants.

In appendix D of Bennett (1975), there is a list and discussion of "Plant Life in Sixteenth-Century Florida." Sixty-two species of trees, 61 shrubs, 18 vines, and more than 300 additional plants are mentioned of which more than 200 could have been in use by the Indians for foods, drinks, medicines, and dyes when the whites came. Some of these are familiar to us, such as grapes, per-

1.44. Front and back views of the owl totem being unloaded at the Florida State Museum in 1955.

simmons, nuts, tobacco, etc. Others, such as the roots of coontie *(Zamia integrifolia)*, were used as flour. The use of roots for food is mentioned extensively in the early historic literature. For example, Fontaneda states that they have "bread of roots which is their common food the greater part of the time but the lake [Okeechobee] rises so high in some seasons that the roots cannot be reached and they are without eating this bread for some time" (True 1944). The identification of specific plants is often difficult. About the only reliable way to conclude if people were ingesting plants, rather than the plants being a natural part of the environment, is through an analysis of human coprolites. Other markers might be indicators of plant manipulation and/or usage. If plants or animals are not familiar food items to individuals who are examining historic documents or the archaeological record, they tend to be ignored. Fontaneda mentions that the Indians preferred deer or fowl, but they also ate eels, alligators, sharks, snakes, rats (probably opossum), tortoises, and "many more disgusting reptiles which, if we were to continue enumerating, we should never be through" (True 1944).

We still know very little about the womb-to-tomb life of Florida Indians. A great deal of speculation about what people were doing prehistorically is based on early historic records. As a matter of fact, many of the sites where a more elaborate way of life existed border on the Historic period so that sometimes it is not clear if the sites are prehistoric, protohistoric, or early historic. Historic records are nice because they name people and events that are not recognizable from the archaeological record, but sometimes they are incomplete, biased, or downright erroneous. Occasionally archaeological data have been able to correct, verify, and supplement written documents. Investigations carried out at St. Augustine are an excellent example.

Two of the most spectacular archaeological investigations in recent years, which have located portions of de Soto's route through Florida, are the excavations at the Tatham site and the discovery of de Soto's 1539–40 winter camp in Tallahassee. Recovered at both of these sites is ample physical evidence of European contact. At the Tatham site, several hundred human burials were found, as were 153 early-sixteenth-century glass beads, and objects of silver, gold, and iron (fig. 1.45). Of the burials, more than 70 were found in the upper portion of the mound, many in association with European artifacts. It is believed that most of these people died of diseases brought by the de Soto expedition. A few skeletons bore evidence of injury and death from sword wounds. The Anhaica site in Tallahassee, located less than a mile from the state capitol, was a principal Apalachee Indian village that was found aban-

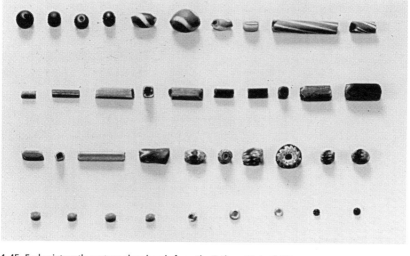

1.45. Early-sixteenth-century glass beads from the Tatham Mound, Citrus County, Florida. (Photograph by Harry W. Buck II; courtesy of Jeffrey M. Mitchem, Arkansas Archaeological Survey.)

0   1   2
cm

doned by de Soto's expedition. De Soto occupied the village and used it as a base for five months. Among the European artifacts recovered when the site was excavated were fragments of Spanish pottery, blown glass beads, and small links of iron (chain mail). More than 90 percent of the items were of aboriginal origin; this is important because if it were not for the few European objects, it would be difficult to determine that the site was of historic age. It was not until later in the Historic period that Indian artifacts began to reflect European influence, such as in new ceramic designs and shapes.

At Hontoon Island we excavated from water-saturated deposits a zone in which all seven major classes of material items—ceramics, stone points, marine shell tools, fauna, flora, cultivated plants, and freshwater shellfish—changed abruptly from those recovered in a slightly older, lower zone. Numerous radiocarbon dates for this drastically different assemblage had a range of error that overlapped with the early sixteenth century, yet European artifacts were not recovered until higher in the deposit. It is difficult to imagine anything except a major environmental or cultural catastrophe that would cause people to modify their way of life as quickly as documented at Hontoon Island. I have proposed that the changes observed were the result of new ideas introduced by refugee Indians who fled brutalities occurring in the Caribbean or further south prior to actual European contact in Florida.

CHRONOLOGY CHART OF THE EARLY CULTURES OF FLORIDA

Date	Name	Major Identifying Features	Location
A.D. 1492+	Historic	European artifacts; decreased populations; written documents	Statewide, especially coastal areas
	Ceramic		
2500 B.P.–A.D. 1492	Late	Regionalism in ceramic styles; burial and temple mounds; bow and arrow late in period; Pinellas and other small stone points; plant cultivation in some areas; ceremonial pottery; trade in nonlocal materials; social complexity	Nearly statewide
3000–2500 B.P.	Middle	Transitional with changes in ceramic pastes, manufacture, and decoration; increasing social complexity; efficient exploitation of aquatic resources; influences from distant cultures	Statewide, especially Gulf Coast
4000–3000 B.P.	Early	First ceramic pots (Orange, fiber-tempered); efficient exploitation of aquatic resources; changes in stone point styles; shell technology diversifies and continues until Historic period	Mostly Atlantic coast and St. Johns River
	Archaic		
6000–4000 B.P.	Late	Shell middens appear along coasts and rivers; small stemmed stone bifaces; marine shell technology becomes major addition to culture; steatite and other imported materials	Statewide, but most evident along rivers and coasts
7000–6000 B.P.	Middle	A variety of stemmed stone bifaces; wetsites with preserved human remains, plants, and wood and bone technology; populations more concentrated; intense use of chert quarries	Statewide; wet sites mostly in South Florida
9000–7000 B.P.	Early	Distinctive stemmed stone bifaces, e.g., Arredondo and Kirk Serrated; Windover expands knowledge of this period (see text)	Nearly statewide, but evidence not abundant

Date	Name	Major Identifying Features	Location
	Paleoindian		
10,000–9000 B.P.	Late and Middle	All modern fauna; Bolen (Late); Suwannee and Simpson (Middle) most common stone bifaces; Harney Flats best stratigraphic evidence at quarry site (see text); period is poorly dated	Nearly statewide, especially rivers and springs
11,500–10,000 B.P.	Early	Butchered bones of Pleistocene animals; Clovis biface; distinctive tools of stone and elephant ivory	Nearly statewide in springs and rivers
Before 11,500 B.P.	Prepaleoindian	Largely unkown; absence of stone bifaces; crude stone tools; butchered bones of Pleistocene animals; wood, bone, and antler tools	Rivers, springs, and stone quarries

We will never know what the Florida Indians would be doing today if their way of life had not been disrupted in the early sixteenth century and eventually obliterated. They seemed to have reached a steady state. Technology that might have led to a more complex society was not present. They used no source of animal power to haul burdens or pull a plow. Bison were abundant in the Southeast, and the Spanish wondered why they were not castrated and used in this manner. The dog was domesticated, and it may have been able to carry a load if harnessed to a **travois** in a method similar to one used among the Plains Indians. No such conveyance is mentioned for Florida. However, the dog was sometimes eaten by the native people of the Southeast.

Fossil fuels were not utilized as an energy source anywhere in the Americas; in fact, only coal was used in the Old World at this time. Water power via the canoe, manufactured from magnificent heart pine, served as the only high-energy source available in Florida. But without sails, the canoes too were powered by human energy or depended on downstream currents instead of wind. The Florida Indians evidently had no knowledge of the wheel since it was not used in the ceramic industry or for any other task. Their pyrotechniques apparently were not well developed. No kilns have been discovered that would have permitted high firing of pottery. Temperature control was needed for altering certain flint artifacts, in the bone and woodworking industries, for cooking, etc., but these methods seem to have remained unchanged for thousands of years. Metals are not native to Florida; thus, the Indians did not develop metallurgical skills. If they had done so, they probably would have been similar to those of South and Central America, where wonderful artifacts of personal adornment were fashioned from gold and silver, but few utilitarian items were made that could provide extrasomatic sources of energy. The pure metals were too soft for that purpose and although alloying was practiced, it was used to enhance the creative effect of the art objects.

Without new technological achievements, the Indians of Florida attempted to elaborate their culture in another way—through their social structure. Certain specializations became prestigious and resulted in a hierarchial society with positions inherited through **matrilineal clans**. More efficient use of time through specialized diversity is a way of building capital. But their surpluses (primarily food) were expended on temple mound building that entailed a labor force that had to be fed and on ceremonialism that also exhausted the surplus food supply. Monument building and ceremonialism may promote *esprit de corps,* but they lead nowhere unless accompanied by technological innovations.

The Spanish could have guided the Indians out of the Stone Age. They wanted to make Catholics of the Indians, but they did not wish them to become too familiar with their firearms and other weapons. In the long run, it did not matter. Their future lay only in the hereafter.

TWO

 SURVEY AND EXCAVATION

Ask an archaeologist "How did you know to dig there?" and the answer might be book-length. In this chapter I will describe (1) some of the circumstances that motivate archaeologists to conduct fieldwork, and (2) the actual mechanics involved in guiding projects through their various stages until they are completed or terminated.

First, it is important to understand that American archaeologists, as anthropologists, wish to learn as much as they are able about cultures that existed in the past. The task is formidable since there are no human survivors to interview, usually no written documents, and only a fraction of the objects used in everyday and ritual activities have withstood the ravages of time. But the archaeological record is fragile for an even more significant reason: it is finite. Comparing the problems faced by the archaeologist to those of an archivist or experimental scientist, Taylor wrote:

> The archivist and the experimental scientist may with impunity select from their sources those facts which have for them a personal and immediate significance in terms of some special problem. Their libraries and experimental facilities may be expected to endure, so that in the future there may be access to the

same or a similar body of data. If, however, it were certain that, after the archivist's first perusal, each document would be utterly and forever destroyed, it would undoubtedly be required of him that he transcribe the entire record rather than just that portion which at the moment interests him. He would have difficulty in justifying his research if, knowingly, he caused the destruction of a unique record for the sake of abstracting only a narrowly selected part.... Therefore, only one objective can be sanctioned with regard to the actual excavation of archaeological sites: that of securing the most complete record possible not only of those details which are of interest to the collector, but of the entire geographic and human environment." (Taylor 1948:154)

Archaeologists destroy as they dig. Once specimens are removed from their context, it is impossible to view them again in their original surroundings. It is only by transposing the archaeological record to notes, maps, sketches, photographs, etc., that it can be preserved for study. Archaeological field and laboratory methods have not been static through the years. They have been refined constantly to incorporate techniques that generate data capable of answering questions about past cultures and environments that formerly were never asked. Because archaeological resources are shrinking at an alarming rate and because archaeologists realize that much untapped information may be contained in sites that remain, there is a tendency to be increasingly cautious about making decisions to excavate.

In the nineteenth and early twentieth centuries, circumstances prevailed in North America that piqued the curiosity of a few individuals about the continent's early inhabitants. Two of the most important of these were: (1) extensive land-clearing activities in the East that continually exposed large quantities of antiquities, and (2) the remains of ancestral structures in areas where Native American groups still resided, particularly in the southwestern states. In fact, Indian studies in the Southwest led to the birth of North American anthropology and archaeology. The information accumulated about archaeological sites and artifacts since at least 1850 furnishes the base upon which regional and temporal prehistories are recognized today. Many archaeological sites are still found by landowners with added input now from state and federal compliance requirements, developers, divers, avocational archaeologists, and problem-oriented investigations. Natural disasters such as earthquakes and floods sometimes expose archaeological sites also. Whether or not a site is excavated by a professional archaeologist depends upon a number of factors that I will detail in this chapter.

Archaeological sites can be placed into three major categories: habitation, special use, and shipwreck sites. Habitation sites include permanent villages or seasonally occupied camps. Special use sites include cemeteries, ceremonial areas, caches, quarries, and more. Shipwrecks, though not as common as habitation and special use sites, are important because they represent a slice of time and an assemblage of materials entombed in death as they were related in life: Pompeii-like conditions.

Traditionally, special use sites, particularly human burial or ceremonial areas, have been studied the most extensively because the largest quantity of unbroken ornate and artistic grave goods or ritual objects are recovered there. Even with today's research-oriented approach and the claim that artifacts have no intrinsic value, a disproportionate amount of grant funds is allocated to excavate these types of sites. Habitation sites generally yield a greater variety of materials pertaining to everyday activities than do special use sites, but the materials are usually broken and/or lack decoration. Investigations of shipwrecks and other types of underwater sites have increased since scuba technology was developed and improved and various types of submersibles have become available. Shipwrecks in Florida, of course, postdate the Columbus voyages.

SURVEY

Most archaeologists today are interested in how people dispersed themselves across the landscape. Therefore, sites are seldom excavated until a regional survey is conducted to assess the overall environmental situation and the land use and settlement patterns of aboriginal inhabitants within a region's ecological zones. It is a logical first step to learn the number, location, and nature of archaeological remains in the area of interest. Preliminary reconnaissance activities are usually carried out prior to a detailed field survey. These activities include an examination of archival materials, site files, photographs, and maps to determine if sites have been recorded in the area already. Aerial photographs can often pinpoint archaeological sites that can be subsequently located on the ground. Local historians and collectors should be consulted, for they are a major source of information that is often neglected. Permission to cross private lands should be obtained and a code of ethics observed, such as closing gates, etc. It goes without saying that money, time, personnel, and equipment must be available before a survey is undertaken.

The importance of the archaeological survey should not be underestimated because it may not be followed by excavations. It is a noninvasive, nondestructive means to assess past human activities in an area that may be destroyed by planned development. Or, in the case of a project with a specific research objective, it may reveal the most advantageous spot to excavate in order to test an investigator's hypotheses. The goal of a surface survey is to produce a reliable prediction about what is under the ground. It is only going to be as good as the methods employed and the people employing them. Once the area and research design have been defined, mapping, remote sensing, and sampling strategies are the keys to a successful archaeological survey.

Maps

As with most things these days, maps have become more complex and diverse. Road and **topographic** maps are probably still the most used and most important. A road map, or a portion thereof, gives the general area where a survey will be conducted, including the state and county (or counties) involved. Quadrangle maps published by the U.S. Geological Survey (USGS), obtainable from some bookstores, give Universal Transverse Mercator (UTM) coordinates, township (T), range (R), section (Sec.) numbers, and elevations above sea level (topographic relief) within a given area. Quadrangles cover 7.5 minutes of latitude and longitude at a scale of 1:24,000 (1 inch:2000 feet; measurements are now usually converted to the metric system).

On the Index to Topographic Maps of Florida it can be seen that the state is divided into more than 1,000 quadrangles. Alachua County is composed of 25 whole or partial quadrangles, and each quadrangle has a name, such as Newberry, Gainesville West, Gainesville East, Orange Heights, Archer, etc. (fig. 2.1). Townships are generally divided into 36 one-square-mile sections, although they are sometimes complicated by Florida land grants. The University of Florida, for example, is located within several sections of the Gainesville East Quadrangle, T10S, R20E, Sec. 6 (primarily) at approximately 29°39'30" north latitude and 82°20'30" west longitude, given in degrees (°), minutes ('), and seconds (") (fig. 2.2).

To be more precise in describing a location, a section can be divided and designated in the following manner: NW$\frac{1}{4}$ of the SW$\frac{1}{4}$ of Section 6 (fig. 2.3). Zones 16 and 17 are the particular east-west segments of UTM coordinates assigned to Florida counties. The easting coordinate is a six-digit number measured in meters eastward from the zone origin. The University of Florida at Gainesville is in Zone 17 with an easting value of approximately 370000E.

2.1. Index to topographic maps of Florida, showing some of the Alachua County quadrangles.

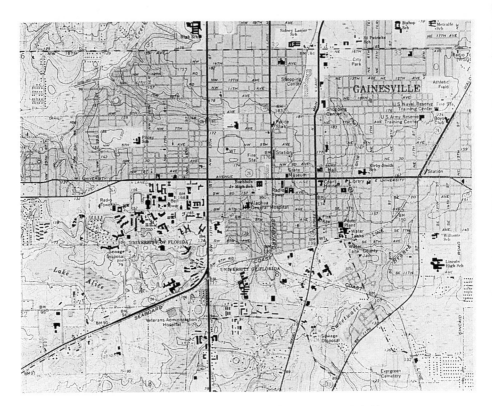

2.2. Gainesville East Quadrangle map, showing the location of the University of Florida.

6	5	4	3	2	1
7	8	9	10	11	12
18	17	16	15	14	13
19	20	21	22	23	24
30	29	28	27	26	25
31	32	33	34	35	36

2.3. Section 6 of a township, showing how a section can be subdivided.

The northing coordinate is a seven-digit number recording the distance north of the equator in meters. The northing value for the University of Florida is approximately 3280000N.

Contour mapping and methods to fix the exact geographic position of a specific spot on a map are discussed below in the excavation section. Many other kinds of maps are used as needed to carry out archaeological projects: navigational maps; real estate plat maps; soils maps; maps showing physiographic, geologic, and hydrologic features; Landsat images, etc.

Remote Sensing

Aerial photography, various magnetic prospecting methods, and side-scan sonar are some of the remote sensing techniques that are being used increasingly in some areas to assist in the discovery of archaeological sites without destroying them in the process. Several of these methods have been used in Florida to conduct archaeological surveys in the Everglades and Big Cypress and at Spanish mission sites, as well as to locate shipwrecks. Remote sensing is most beneficial in places where archaeologists hope to find structures, buried irrigation systems, extensive agricultural lands, shipwrecks, and other objects or edifices that may now lie below the ground or underwater. These techniques are often very expensive, they are not always reliable, and they usually furnish only a general picture of what might be present. Nearly all remote sensing techniques must be followed up with some kind of additional testing (ground truth) to provide more detailed information. Nevertheless, there are occasions when these methods are extremely useful and they may be the only investigation that is conducted.

Archaeology has benefited from aviation and aerial photography since World War I, with contributions from such famous persons as Charles Lindbergh. Technological advances made during World War II and space explorations have also been utilized by archaeologists. Sites that have left almost no surface trace on the ground have been found on aerial photographs. From the air, one can look down and view the earth as a whole in ways that are not possible by any other means. The Landsat series, or NASA Earth Resources Technology Satellite (ERTS-1), map of Florida has a scale of 1:500,000 (1 cm equals 5 km or about 3+ miles). The false color imagery of this map shows cleared areas as white or light gray, vegetation as shades of red, urban areas as blue-gray, and open water in shades of blue. Because of the nature of archaeological remains in Florida and because vegetation grows so rapidly, aerial photography, especially the small scale of the Landsat series, may not be as applicable here as elsewhere.

Geophysical remote sensing devices involve either passing energy of various kinds through the soil in order to "read" what lies below the surface from the anomalies encountered by the energy or measuring the intensity of the earth's magnetic field. Echo sounding or seismic methods can be simple, such as dowsing, in which the ground is struck with a heavy object and the experienced ear detects resonant differences indicating buried objects. Many other sonic, radio wave (ground-penetrating radar), and electrical impulse techniques have been utilized depending upon availability and applicability. The discovery of underwater sites, particularly shipwrecks, has increased greatly in the last few years through the use of the proton magnetometer, side-scan sonar, and the sub-bottom profiler, which have been valuable in detecting and mapping objects and features on and below the seafloor.

Electrical resistivity is a technique based on the principle that the damper the soil the more easily it will conduct electricity (low resistivity). If, for example, a stone wall is encountered, the instrument will measure higher resistivity.

Buried features containing even minute amounts of iron produce slight but measurable distortions in the earth's magnetic field. The proton magnetometer is the instrument most commonly used to locate buried hearths, pottery kilns, iron objects, pits, and ditches by magnetic detection. The principle is simple. Grains of iron oxide in clay, randomly oriented if unfired, will line up and become permanently fixed when heated to about 700°C (1292°F) or more. This phenomenon has also been used as a dating method (see chapter 4). Anomalies caused by pits or ditches occur because the magnetic susceptibility of their contents is greater than that of the surrounding subsoil.

Metal detectors are electromagnetic devices helpful in detecting metals and other buried remains. They also are used by nonarchaeologists to find and plunder sites.

In summary, nondestructive remote sensing methods have been used to locate buried sites and features, to determine the geographic extent of sites, and to produce contour maps. Most of these techniques are expensive and require the services of trained personnel to operate and interpret them.

Sampling

We are still left with the questions of where sites exist that hold the greatest potential for furnishing the most significant information about the past, which sites are the least disturbed, which sites are in the greatest danger of being disturbed, and at which sites the landowners are receptive to excavation. In the case of problem-oriented research, we wish to learn which site or sites will answer the questions being addressed about a specific culture, a specific cultural activity, a specific time period, or a general investigation of habitation in the area throughout all time periods. Excavations should not be conducted before there is abundant and exact information.

Archaeologists have always used sampling techniques prior to actual excavations, but in the past their methods tended to be **nonprobabilistic**. Fieldwork concentrated on conspicuous sites (e.g., Mayan pyramids) or conveniently located sites (e.g., next to roads) and/or depended on the intuition or experience of the archaeologist. This type of sampling is fine for many specific tasks if it is truly representative of the **data universe**, but usually it is not. For instance, generations of archaeologists studying Mayan culture excavated large temple structures and ignored investigations that would provide insights about how the peasants lived. Closer to home, generations of archaeologists in Florida studied Ceramic period cultures, while six to eight thousand years of Paleoindian and Archaic activites were virtually neglected. In order to judge in any quantitative manner how representative the sample is of a site or region (the data universe), some form of statistical or **probabilistic sampling** needs to be used. This type of approach allows researchers to project the total number and size of sites. Use of probabilistic sampling techniques has reached new heights in the last 20 years of the twentieth century because of the necessity to do the best job possible with the limited time and money allotted for emergency salvage or cultural resource management (CRM) projects conducted prior to modifications resulting from development (see chapter 6).

Sampling strategies look good on paper but in reality are often difficult to apply in the field because of impassable terrain, hostile landowners, politics, etc. For a clear discussion and definitions of terminology associated with statistical sampling, see Fagan (1991:198–203). Once the universe is defined and a grid of square sampling units is imposed over it (see excavation section below), archaeologists generally use one of three basic sampling types:

Simple random sampling, like drawing cards from a hat, randomly selects for sampling a certain number of units in the grid frame (a table of random numbers is usually used). All samples are treated as equal without taking into account variables such as topography. This method is useful if no previous archaeological work has been conducted in the area.

Systematic sampling, in which one unit is selected and then others are chosen at equal intervals from the first one; for example, every fifth square on a grid of equal-sized squares.

Stratified sampling is probably the most useful method when sample units are not uniform, such as different environmental settings. This type of sampling permits intensive examination of some parts of the grid frame and less detailed work on other areas where, for example, experience has shown that investigations will not be productive. Sampling strategies are important for predicting where sites will not be found as well as where they will be found. It is logical to expect that people utilized areas where resources needed for survival were located, such as food, water, and raw materials.

Most archaeologists do not have the training to interpret the findings of most remote sensing techniques, to draw sophisticated detailed and scaled maps, or to conduct statistical analyses. Many archaeological projects today include the services and skills of cartographers and statisticians as well as other experts.

Despite the real and hypothetical data derived from written documents, maps, remote sensing, and grandiose sampling techniques, archaeologists must verify the evidence by physically walking and conducting surface and often subsurface inspections and/or collections of artifacts. This is done to determine the significance of a site or area in providing new information about the past or to delineate major cultural remains that will be impacted by impending development. Surface collections made within sampling units enable the archaeologist to plot densities of artifacts and features and to assess the antiquity of occupation. There is always the question of how reliable surface collections are in predicting what is under the ground. Old sites or **multicomponent** sites might not be recognized at all. In order to determine the relationship between surface and subsurface deposits, it is often necessary to probe, auger, core, shovel, or dig test pits. All information derived from the field survey should be recorded and mapped precisely on survey forms. The information may be used to determine where subsequent excavations will take place, or it may substitute for excavation if further fieldwork is not recommended.

Survey data forms must be devised that furnish accurate information about the location of sites (state, county, quadrangle map, township, range, section), ownership, purpose of the survey, physiographic situation (vegetation, soil, contour elevation), what sites are already recorded, history of past activity at sites, previous designations and publications if any, present condition of sites, site limits (horizontal and vertical if sites are tested), sketch map, photos, aboriginal features or artifacts observed, comments and/or recommendations, date of survey, and name of recorder. A Survey Log Sheet is illustrated in chapter 6.

EXCAVATION

Archaeological field manuals are valuable in furnishing general ideas about how to excavate systematically, but there are many kinds of sites in the world and every site is unique. "So varied are the skills of the excavator that much of a professional archaeologist's training in the field is obtained as a graduate student working at routine tasks and gaining experience in the methods of excavating and site survey under experienced supervision" (Fagan 1991:216).

2.4. Air photo of the Groves Orange Midden site, Lake Monroe, Volusia County, Florida (summer 1993), showing an example of how archaeologists overcome adverse conditions in order to excavate significant cultural remains. In this case, two locations in the lake were cofferdammed and a well point system installed to keep the lake water out of the units while excavations proceeded systematically. Individuals are working 2 meters below the lake bed. Thousands of water-saturated organic specimens, which usually do not survive, furnished important information about diet and environment in this area of Florida 6,000 years ago.

Archaeological fieldwork should not be carried out unless an individual has first had an opportunity to work with a qualified archaeologist. A surveying course in civil engineering is recommended also. The fieldworker should know enough to be properly prepared, but even the most well-informed fieldworkers should proceed as if they are ignorant of what will be encountered. Important observations might be missed if a previous knowledge of what lies beneath the ground is assumed. In addition, archaeologists should be able to adapt excavation techniques to the field situation (fig. 2.4).

Countless descriptions of field methods exist in the literature. The most important advice is: DO IT RIGHT! Since sites are recorded precisely, they could conceivably be plotted on a map of the world and, unless obliterated by natural or cultural events, be found again anytime in the future. For example, several years ago a graduate student was preparing to conduct new investigations at a site dug in the 1940s by Dr. Charles H. Fairbanks. Taking Fairbanks's field notes and sketches, the student was able to locate the exact corners of one of his old excavation units. Regrettably, many people believe that the sole requirements for archaeological fieldwork are

> picks and shovels, strong backs, and a place to dig. Unfortunately this over-simplification is difficult to refute because at first blush fieldwork doesn't seem to require much beyond interest and leisure time. But fieldwork . . . is of utmost and crucial importance because it is here that the control of the information begins and ends. . . . It is correct, however, to think of fieldwork as a series of techniques and procedures that are neither difficult nor profound. It is the invisible background of guiding concepts, assumptions, and scientific principles that the observer and recorder possesses as professional intellectual equipment that marks the difference between the archaeologist and the antiquarian or mere collector. (Jennings 1989:29)

The site or sites that promise to offer the most information are the ones that should be selected for excavation. The reasons for excavating should be based on the significance of the archaeological remains with regard to (1) local, national, or international importance; (2) quantity, quality, or uniqueness; (3) threat of destruction; and (4) public interest. In other words, priorities should be established. The preliminary survey and sampling procedures should have furnished an estimation of what percentage of a site should be excavated in order to obtain a representative sample of the universe. There are occasions when total excavation of a site is recommended, but selective excavation is usually practiced because (1) most sites are too large to consider total excavation; (2) time, money, and personnel are not available; or (3) a portion of the site is saved for the future when there may be better techniques or a new set of questions may be answered by the remaining deposits. All Florida archaeologists today wish that C.B. Moore had observed this last policy in the late nineteenth century when he "demolished" (his word) dozens of mounds.

As stressed above, there are many kinds and sizes of sites located in diverse geographic and topographic settings all over the world. Each site will require a different mapping and excavation strategy. The archaeologist may need the services of a professional surveyor to overcome problems associated with distance, direction, terrain, etc., and to tie the site into a permanent benchmark (BM). In this section, I describe and illustrate basic procedures of mapping and excavaton, including equipment and record keeping.

Field Methods and Equipment

Primary requisites for digging are the establishment of a **datum point** for horizontal control and a **datum plane** for vertical control. Both datum point and datum plane should be permanent markers and/or tied to permanent designations such as USGS benchmarks. The datum point is the position from which all horizontal measurements will be made. Obviously, if its location is lost or it is not recorded precisely, the primary objective of excavations is lost also—that is, *the systematic recovery of archaeological remains*—and it is virtually impossible to attach any chronological significance to the materials. The datum plane can be conceived of as a horizontal sheet extending over the site and clearing its highest point. It is used as a reference in measuring elevation. The datum plane should be assigned an arbitrary round figure (e.g., 10 meters, 100 meters) unless its elevation in relationship to sea level can be accurately determined.

Surveying instruments, such as transits or theodolites, are recommended for contour mapping or for gridding a site. These are expensive and delicate precision instruments having telescopic sights for measuring horizontal and vertical (elevation) angles by means of cross hairs and stadia hairs that are mounted in the telescope (fig. 2.5). The surveying instrument is used in conjunction with a leveling or stadia rod to read distances and elevations. The rod is marked with graduated 10-mm (1-cm) measurements along its length with zero at the bottom. Each graduation is .01 meter (1 cm) wide (fig. 2.6). The erectly held rod is sighted through the telescope of the instrument. Distance is measured by determining the difference x 100 between the top and

2.5. Students being instructed in the use of the transit during field school: (top) at the Container Corporation of America site, Marion County, 1975; (bottom) at Hontoon Island, Volusia County, 1984.

bottom readings of the two parallel stadia hairs that are mounted in the telescope of the surveying instrument. If the top stadia hair reading is 6.0 and the bottom is 5.0, the distance from the datum point to the rod is 100 meters (6.0–5.0 = 1.0 x 100 = 100). Elevation is read by noting the measurment on the graduated rod at which the horizontal cross hair of the instrument intersects the face of the rod and subtracting that figure from the datum plane (100) and the height of the instrument. For example, if the figure read on the stadia rod is 7.0 m and the height of the instrument is 1.5 m, then the elevation would be 94.5, or 5.5 m below datum (BD): 100 + 1.5 = 101.5–7.0 = 94.5.

It must be remembered that the height of the instrument will change whenever the instrument is moved and will need to be refigured each time. There are ways to avoid this situation, especially if there is going to be only one transit station at a site. When the station is set up for the first time, the datum plane can be designated by sighting on a tree, boulder, barn, house, or other immovable object and marking the place on the structure where the cross hair intersects with something visible, such as a brightly painted nail. Thereafter, the datum plane can be established quickly each morning when the transit is

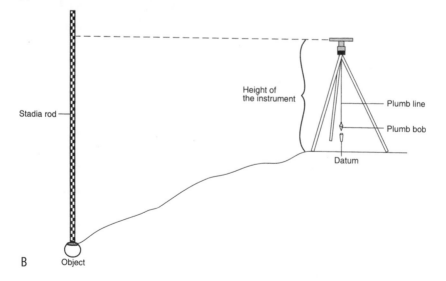

2.6. (a) Using stadia rod at Lake Monroe (note differences in strata); (b) illustration of the use of the transit and stadia rod to measure elevation.

A

Height of
the instrument

Plumb line

Plumb bob

Stadia rod

Datum

B   Object

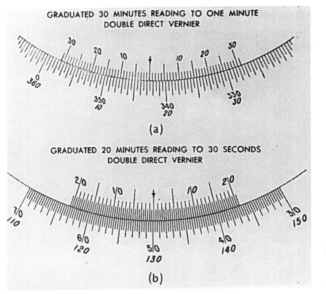

GRADUATED 30 MINUTES READING TO ONE MINUTE
DOUBLE DIRECT VERNIER

(a)

GRADUATED 20 MINUTES READING TO 30 SECONDS
DOUBLE DIRECT VERNIER

2.7. Vernier scale.

(b)

set up or can be checked periodically throughout the day to see if the instrument has remained accurate. The height of the instrument varies because it rests on the legs of a tripod. Pounding a stake at the outside position of each tripod leg after the instrument is in place the first time makes it easier to set up the same way the next time, but the height of the instrument must still be verified by the datum plane marker or by backsighting from a known elevation. The transit or theodolite must be absolutely level whenever distance or elevation is measured. Surveying instruments are equipped with bubble levels and leveling screws for this purpose, and only hands-on practice can provide the experience necessary to get the hang of leveling.

These days theodolites can be equipped with laser beams that cut recording times by 50 percent and increase accuracy as much as 500 percent. A small microprocessor records the measurement data, and a small field computer unloads its data into a personal computer that processes the measurements and produces a color-coded diagram of the day's work. Infrared and laser radiation devices, such as electro-optical distance measuring (EDM) equipment and the Auto-Ranger instrument, measure anything from a few meters to several miles and provide the archaeologist with both accuracy and speed. Such sophisticated equipment is very expensive and is rarely available for archaeological projects. In most cases, distance and elevation can be determined with a measuring tape, line level, and plumb bob, but care must be taken to hold the tape taut and level.

In the United States, the **sexagesimal system** is used to measure angles. This system divides angles into 360°; each degree is divided into 60 minutes; and each minute is divided into 60 seconds. (The centesimal scale is used in Europe.) The surveying instrument is equipped with a compass (vernier scale) by which angles can be measured (fig. 2.7). The instrument is set up and, with the aid of a plumb bob, leveled directly over the point marked on the datum stake from which all horizontal measurements will be taken. The most ideal situation is to orient the grid system in a north-south, east-west position and fix the compass at 0° (360°) in the direction of true north. All angles (**bearings**) then will be measured in relationship to true north (the meridian or fixed line of reference). True north is a line passing through the geographic north and south poles in relation to the site point. It differs from magnetic north, which is *north* as indicated by a magnetic compass. The direction of magnetic north changes with time and is therefore not as desirable a reference point as true north. But true north is not always easy to establish and sometimes an *assumed* north is used, which is an arbitrary measurement as close as possible to the true meridian.

Datum has been established, the surveying instrument is set up, and the site is ready to be gridded. The grid is composed of two sets of intersecting parallel lines, each set intersecting the other at right angles. Stakes are driven under the intersects of the lines and a small nail on the top of the stake marks the exact intersect that will be used as a local datum to record the **three-dimensional** location of finds in a specific unit.

An ideal way to grid is as follows: Locate the datum to the southwest and outside of the area where excavations will take place and label it 0 N, 0 E. All horizontal measurements will be made in relation to this location. On a map, the conventional symbol for the datum point is a cross within a circle. In our example, we are going to grid a small site (25 m x 25 m) into 5-meter squares (fig. 2.8). The location of the grid is superimposed on a large area already surveyed and mapped (see below). It was chosen because the heaviest concentration of artifacts was found there when surface collections were made. The vernier on the transit is zeroed at true north and locked. North is designated on a map with an arrow pointing in that direction. The instrument man and rod man work together to establish the coordinates either by sighting through the instrument to determine distance or by using a tape. A stake (about 30+ cm long and pointed at one end) is driven along the north grid line every 5 meters and each stake is marked: 5 N, 30 E; 10 N, 30 E; 15 N, 30 E; 20 N, 30 E; 25 N, 30 E. The transit is then rotated 90° and locked at due east,

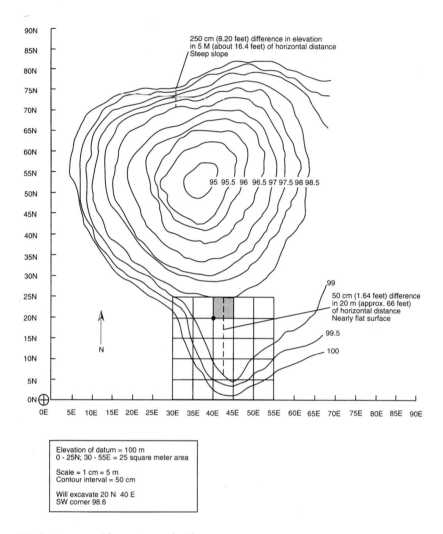

2.8. Contour map with superimposed grid.

and the process is continued with the eastward lying stakes numbered 0 N, 35 E; 0 N, 40 E; 0 N, 45 E; 0 N, 50 E; 0 N, 55 E.

If the archaeologist intends to excavate the entire 25 m x 25 m area, then each 5-meter unit must be staked and the elevation of each stake recorded in relation to the already established datum plane. On the site map each 5-meter unit can be either assigned a number from 1 to 25 or designated by its coordinates; e.g., 20 N, 40 E. If only one or a few units are to be excavated, then it is not necessary to record the elevation of each division of the grid. The stake located in the southwest corner of each unit to be excavated should contain its bearing and elevation: e.g., 20 N, 40 E, 98.6 (or 1.4 m below datum— BD). When excavations are taking place in that unit, the locations of artifacts, features, etc., should be measured from the southwest stake (fig. 2.9). For example, in the field notebook it may be recorded that "a stone spearhead was found 2.4 N, 3 E from the southwest corner of unit 20 N, 40 E (or 22.4 N, 43 E of datum), at 1.8 BD" (the elevation of the stake plus 0.4 m deeper in the unit). This information will also be written on the container in which the specimen is stored. While measurements can be made from the other corner stakes, it is best to remain consistent and record everything in relation to one point to avoid confusion.

This three-dimensional measurement is most commonly achieved in the following manner: A metal or cloth metric tape is oriented north-south from the position at the southwest stake where the coordinates for that stake were recorded. The tape is extended north until it intersects at a right angle another tape that is oriented east-west over the object encountered **in situ**. A plumb bob and string hung above the object locates the artifact precisely, and a bubble (line) level is used to obtain an accurate depth below datum. A top and bottom measurement might be taken if an object or feature is fairly large, such as a pottery bowl or a fire hearth. If all materials collected from one level

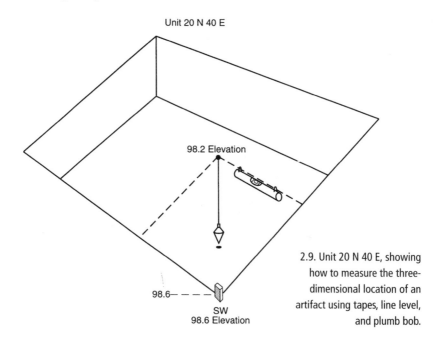

Unit 20 N 40 E

98.2 Elevation

98.6

SW
98.6 Elevation

2.9. Unit 20 N 40 E, showing how to measure the three-dimensional location of an artifact using tapes, line level, and plumb bob.

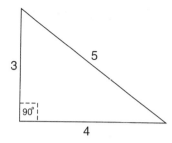

2.10. How to establish a right angle (90°).

of a unit are similar and very abundant, such as 200 flint chips, then they can be placed together in a specimen bag labeled with that particular unit and level without plotting the exact location for each chip. This same procedure is followed if an item is dislodged accidentally from its **matrix** and it is not possible to record its precise coordinates.

The transit can be used to turn right angles, but the task of setting up the transit for each reading becomes cumbersome and time consuming. Right angles can be measured with a tape by using the Pythagorean principle of the proportions of a 3–4–5 right triangle. A perpendicular line can be positioned by measuring a 3-meter distance (or multiple of 3) along a straight line, a 4-meter distance (or multiple of 4) in the direction of the intended perpendicular from one end of the 3-meter measurement, and a 5-meter distance (or multiple of 5) from the other end of the 3-meter measurement to the top of the 4-meter distance (fig. 2.10).

Elevations are recorded for reasons other than for the vertical control of stratigraphy, features, and artifacts during excavations. When the elevation of each grid stake has been determined, a topographic map can be prepared that gives the shape of the site's surface or the shapes of particular structures within a site, such as mounds. Topographic maps of a region, usually prepared during surveys, are designed to show the relationship of an archaeological site to the local physiographic environment: lakes, rivers, streams, hills, needed resources, etc. Surface elevations and depressions are represented by a system of contour lines, i.e., lines connecting points of the same elevation. If, for example, one contour interval extends a horizontal distance of 20 meters, a fairly flat surface is indicated. On the other hand, if the contour intervals are spaced close together, a steep slope is indicated. All measurements are transferred to graph paper. The scale of the drawing (horizontal distance) and the contour interval (vertical distance) must be noted and are dependent upon the size of the area being mapped (see figs. 2.8 and 2.11). Contour mapping can now be done by computer.

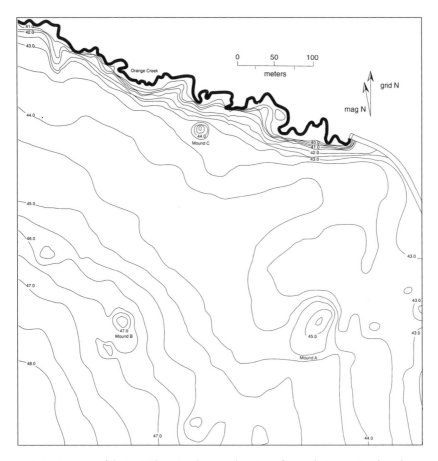

2.11. Contour map of the McKeithen site, showing elevations of mounds, Orange Creek, and other features. (Courtesy of J. T. Milanich.)

In our "ideal" sample grid, all measurements were taken north and east of an established datum. It should be mentioned that the grid system is flexible and that the same datum can be used if for some reason an archaeologist decides to expand excavations to the northwest, southwest, or southeast.

Before excavation begins, all items needed (or anticipated) to ensure that the project will proceed smoothly should be assembled. The list is nearly limitless and will not be the same for every site. Digging and clearing tools include root cutters, machetes, axes, saws, hammers, wheelbarrows, dustpans, shovels, trowels, brooms, brushes, dental picks, and water and air hoses, etc. Even backhoes are used sometimes, and pumps may be required if excavations extend below the water table. Screens of various mesh sizes must be on hand. Recording materials include cameras, measuring tapes, drawing board, graph paper, waterproof notebooks, record sheets, waterproof labels and marking pens, pencils, etc. Containers include various sizes of bags (ziplock or with ties), vials, boxes, and vats (if waterlogged artifacts are expected). Prior to excavations, a recording system must be devised and rigidly adhered to throughout the project (see below for examples).

Essential also is the choice of an area to put the backdirt. It is important to place the backdirt close enough to a unit so that it can be used to refill the hole when excavations are completed, but care should be taken not to cover stakes or an area that has been chosen (or may be chosen) for subsequent exploration. Some circumstances may require that backdirt be carted away by wheelbarrow and returned the same way later on for refilling.

Provisions should be made for inclement weather; for example, large sheets of heavy plastic should be on hand to cover the excavation units in case of rain. Depending upon the number of personnel available, individuals should be assigned the responsibility for specific tasks so they are not neglected throughout each day. Tasks include excavating, note taking, photographing, mapping features and stratigraphy, labeling bags, sorting materials, and more. One person usually attends to several of these chores unless a field school is being held or a project is being assisted by local volunteers. In the case of a field school, duties are rotated daily to give students experience with each task. Arrangements must be made ahead of time for storing equipment and excavated materials so they will be protected while in the field and for transporting them safely at the end of the project. Personal comfort and health should be taken into consideration: bathroom facilities (usually a portable toilet), toilet paper, first aid kit, sunscreen, insect spray (bugs love archaeologists), weed killers (for plants like poison oak or ivy), towels, drinking water, etc. Shades should be erected if people will be working in an open area during the hot season. Food and lodging must be provided if the project is taking place away from home.

The notebook is the archaeologist's bible (supplemented in modern times with video cameras, tape recorders, and computers). A surveyor's notebook with one side cross-sectioned for drawing artifacts or maps to scale is recommended. It contains nearly the entire history of the site, a day-by-day account of activities, and rough sketches of interesting artifacts, features, or stratigraphy. Notes must be written legibly with a no. 2 pencil or a waterproof pen.

[I]t must be remembered that a site is in a larger sense itself an artifact, resulting from human activity. Under most circumstances digging destroys this artifact, and it is therefore necessary that the archaeologist record by means of notes as complete a description as possible ... ever mindful that his observations will be the only source available once excavation has been completed.... The notes should be a record of technique as well as of results, so that future work may be guided by the achievements or errors of a particular dig. (Heizer 1966:49)

A typical day might be recorded as follows:

Site name and number:	Recorder: Jane Doe
Date and Time: Friday, 6–10–94 (8 am)	Weather: Sunny, cool
Crew:	
Unit and beginning level:	
Bag numbers:	
Comments:	
Visitors:	

Now all provisions have been assembled, mapping has been completed, labeled stakes surround the unit to be excavated, and screens are in place over the area chosen to accommodate the backdirt. Vegetation must be cleared in a fairly wide area around the unit if it hinders the ability to read distances and elevations with either the transit or a tape or if it prevents setting up screens and a platform where materials will be sorted and bagged. There must be plenty of room for people to stand. Clearing sometimes includes cutting down small trees but this is avoided whenever possible. At all times, care should be taken not to injure or remove rare plant species, especially in Florida's state parks.

"So many considerations can affect the plan of excavation that it is doubtful if any archaeologist has ever employed exactly the same system twice" (Heizer 1966:39). The kind of site being investigated definitely influences excavation procedures. Trenching provides a way to view a representative cross-section of a site and involves excavating a lineally connected series of excavation units (squares). Excavations can be expanded if features are encountered along the distance of the trench. Trenches can be L-shaped also, and more than one trench or additional units might be dug to verify the representativeness of the first trench. I excavated a long trench, with successful results, from the top of a hill to a sinkhole area at a large chert quarry site in Marion County, Florida. And at Hontoon Island, a trench extended from the top of the undisturbed terrestrial portion of a shell midden into a lagoon where excavations continued in water-saturated deposits (fig. 2.12). Trenching is not usually a desirable technique at sites where extensive features, such as structures, are encountered because it cannot furnish a broad view of the situation.

The quartering or quadrant method is used sometimes to excavate mounds. The mound is separated by **balks** (earth partitions) into four quadrants. Excavation of each quadrant proceeds systematically, and the coordinate balks preserve the contour and stratification of the deposit (fig. 2.13a). Figure 2.13b shows the use of balks at the McKeithen site.

The unit level or box-grid type of excavation described below cannot be used for very deep sites because of the danger of cave-ins and the difficulty of moving dirt from the square to the sorting table or screen. The walls of deep units can be sloped inward to prevent cave-ins or, better still, a large area can be reduced with depth by a method called step-trenching. Archaeologists should always be aware that walls can collapse, especially those composed of loosely consolidated sediments. Crew and visitors should be cautioned to stand back from the edge of the excavation unit (fig. 2.14)

2.12. (a) Transect; (b) excavated trench. Hontoon Island, 1984.

2.13. (a) Examples of leaving balks during excavations;
(b) the use of balks at the McKeithen site. (Courtesy of J. T. Milanich.)

A

B

2.14. Standing back from the edge of the excavation unit to prevent cave-in at Hontoon Island, 1988.

Continuing with our idealized example, let us excavate square 20 N 40 E of our established grid. It is a 5-meter square, but we want to leave a .5-meter balk on all sides; therefore, the actual area to be excavated is 4 meters. The balk can be removed later. Using this method, the corner stakes are kept far enough away from the unit being excavated to protect them from being knocked out of position. Remember that they are used to record precise horizontal and vertical distances. Vegetation has been cleared at the site, but now it is necessary to remove roots and other debris within the unit. This is often not an easy task and must be done with care so as not to rearrange the position of the archaeological materials. Root cutters, axes, shovels, and trowels are employed. Roots may sometimes extend the entire depth of a square but they should *never* be pulled out. They are cut level by level. If there are too many roots and systematic recovery of information is impossible, the unit may be abandoned and excavation moved elsewhere. Even though the top level is usually disturbed, vegetation and soil are screened after they are loosened in case artifacts might be present.

The 4-meter area can be split into four 2-meter (or eight 1-meter) divisions. We have found this approach to be advantageous for a number of reasons:

1. If the unit proves to be culturally sterile, work can be discontinued after one section is completed. Time, money, and personnel are usually limited and should not be wasted on nonproductive units solely for the purpose of moving soil around.

2. Excavations are customarily conducted in 10-cm arbitrary levels unless previously procured core samples or shovel tests have furnished data about the cultural and/or natural stratigraphy (see section on stratigraphy below for a discussion of nonarbitrary excavations). The **profile** produced on the balk by digging 10-cm levels in the first 2-meter division of the unit can be used as a guide to zones of natural or cultural stratigraphy if they exist and are visible. Excavations of the other three divisions can proceed by zones and levels within zones.

3. The smaller the excavation unit, the better control one has over horizontal and vertical locations, and the less damage or displacement of materials is done by trampling.

Elevations are recorded for each corner and the middle of the area to be excavated. After problems with the roots are solved, elevations are taken again to determine how much of the 10 cm is left to excavate in level 1. Checking elevations will be a major exercise throughout the project. Without vertical control, there is no way to pinpoint the location of finds within a unit. Square-ended shovels are used to skim the entire surface of the square, making sure that skimming includes the corners and that the walls are kept at a right angle to the floor. The shovel is never plunged downward. When straightening the walls, care should be taken not to mix levels. For example, if level 4 is being excavated, do not start at level 1 and slice all the way down to level 4. Trowels or brushes replace the shovel if an object or feature is encountered.

Once excavations start, all other tasks begin also. The location of the unit, elevations of the stakes, and other information must be entered in the notebook; bags must be labeled; people must be at the screens; and someone must be prepared to draw scaled **planviews** and stratigraphic profiles as the project progresses.

Labeling Bags and Other Containers

Some archaeologists prefer to write only the site name and a field specimen (FS) number on bags. The FS numbers and the contents of the bags are described on FS cards, which can be referred to later when the materials are analyzed. The FS cards also give the location and level of the unit. This method is okay if there is no danger of bags and cards being separated and if not too long a time elapses before materials are analyzed. A single FS bag usually holds the contents of an entire level; i.e., all artifacts and ecofacts regardless of material.

I use a method that might be considered overkill. I write all pertinent information on the bag including site name and designation, date, unit, quadrant, zone, level, bag number, specimen type, and initials of the individual who sorted the material. For example:

Site name:
8-VO-5000   6–10–94
15N 10E/SW/Z III/L4/Bag 25/wood
                    BP

If the precise coordinates for an artifact or feature have been recorded, as in our example above (22.4 N 43 E, 1.8 BD), they are entered on the bag also. Bags can be numbered consecutively for each quadrant or for each entire unit. The system should remain as open ended as possible. I have always tried to segregate and catalog specimens as quickly as possible. The categories that we have found to cover the full range of materials usually recovered at prehistoric sites in Florida are stone, pottery, shell, wood, bone, artifacts, and miscellaneous (created to encompass such things as seeds and nuts, clay lumps, and other items that do not fit into one of the other groupings). The number of categories increases at Historic period sites. The information is written on the bag with a waterproof marking pen. A piece of waterproof paper or label enclosed in the bag also contains the information, as does a waterproof tag attached to the bag after it is closed by either ziplock or a twist tie. These precautions were born from experience. A laboratory notebook records a day-by-day listing of all bags and their contents.

Screening and Sorting

Materials can be transferred to screens or sorting boards in several ways, depending upon the field situation. They can be shoveled onto the screen directly from the square or they can be shoveled into a wheelbarrow and taken to a separate screening area. In our example, material will be shoveled into a small bucket, carried a short distance to the screen and dumped. There are as many kinds of screening and sorting arrangements as there are archaeological sites. We use three mesh sizes to screen material, $\frac{1}{2}$-inch, $\frac{1}{4}$-inch, and $\frac{1}{8}$-inch, stacked one on the other with the largest mesh at the top (fig. 2.15). If the

2.15. Three-tiered screen set-up used at Lake Monroe. Top screen has $^1/_2$-inch mesh; middle screen, $^1/_4$-inch mesh; and bottom screen, $^1/_8$-inch mesh.

deposits are dry, the loose dirt will fall or shake right through, but if they are wet, hoses will be necessary to separate the dirt or mud from other material. The ½-inch mesh is examined first, and all observable objects are collected and placed in their appropriate bags. Large bones, pottery sherds, spearheads, hickory nuts, etc., are usually found in the ½-inch screen. The ¼-inch screen is then examined, and objects that have passed through the ½-inch mesh are collected and bagged. The ⅛-inch mesh is examined quickly for seeds, beads, and other items of interest. Tiny bones, botanical materials, and the relative amount of each component present will be easier to examine when column samples are analyzed. Column samples will be taken from the wall of each unit after excavations in that unit are completed (see below).

When screening and sorting are completed and the excavators signal that they are ready to begin a new level, all bags from the old level are closed. Bottom elevations for level 1 (top of level 2) are recorded in the notebook, new bags are made out, and the screens are washed to prevent mixing materials from more than one level. Excavations continue in this manner until culturally sterile subsoil or bedrock is reached. If possible, the underlying sediments should be examined using a soil auger or a posthole digger, but generally an archaeologist familiar with the geology of a region can recognize deposits that predate human occupation.

Features

Features are objects or structures encountered during excavations that are considered atypical or are too large to be removed for later analysis: a cache of pottery bowls or spearheads, fire hearths, storage pits, and human burials. Features are numbered consecutively in the order that they are found. They are either **pedestaled** or excavated carefully using trowels, brushes, and even dental picks. Features are often very shallow and if care is not taken, they can be excavated away before they are recorded. Too often, features are recognized only after they have been partially or totally removed or destroyed. When in doubt, call it a feature and photograph and sketch it.

The feature is first mapped in planview (i.e., its horizontal coordinates as if one is looking straight down at it) by using the datum stake and measuring tape to record its exact position and shape. A real or imaginary grid can be placed over the object and a scaled drawing made. The feature can be left in situ and excavations continued around it, which results in a pedestal. When the vertical dimensions have been recorded, the object can be removed and the pedestal excavated. If the feature extends into the level below or into an adjacent unit (people did not live in 4-meter squares), the pedestal is not removed until all dimensions and associations are recorded.

Human burials are a special kind of feature. The dead are not so dead to the archaeologist. In death, all people do not mingle together in one common dust. The elites of the past often distinguished themselves by being buried with unique grave goods or in special places or positions.

> It is obvious that non-perishable items of shell, bone, and stone which are worn as ornaments ... will remain.... Therefore, valuable clues may be gained by observing the exact location of such objects.... For example, necklaces may be indicated by beads, etc. found around the neck and shoulders.... Ornaments are not infrequently placed in the hands and mouth.... One item often not recognized by beginners is powdered red ocher, which is occasionally found with burials. In this form the red ocher stains the bones a dull brick red color and may stain the soil surrounding the bones.... it should be recorded as a burial association. (Heizer 1966:63)

And the dead are not so dead to the physical anthropologist who studies their bones to learn their sex, age of death, health and nutrition, and injuries. If the bones are fragile and time is limited, the entire pedestaled burial can be removed, jacketed in plaster or wrapped carefully, and sent back to the laboratory to be excavated.

Stratigraphy

When the first excavation unit in our example has been completed, the archaeologist dampens and smooths the vertical profile in order to determine if any differences in color, texture, or composition can be observed. If no visible changes are apparent, then excavations must continue by arbitrary 10-cm levels because there may be chronological differences in the deposits even though they appear homogeneous. Samples from each level analyzed by a soil scientist might reveal changes in deposition through time. Usually natural or cultural differences can be detected. If differences are readily distinguishable, they can be divided into zones. A single stratigraphic zone may be a meter or more thick. In this situation, in subsequent excavations, the zone should be divided into arbitrary 10-cm levels and recorded as zone I, level 1, 2, 3, etc.; zone II, level 1, 2, 3, etc.; and so on, to maintain chronological control. Stratigraphy should be photographed and recorded accurately using the datum stake, tape, and plumb bob as already described (horizontal and vertical measurements).

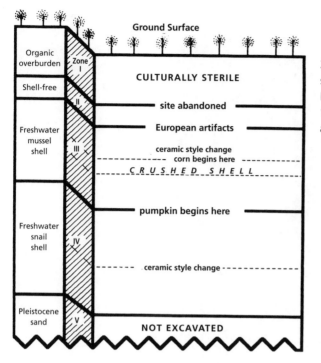

Organic overburden

Zone I

CULTURALLY STERILE

Shell-free

II

━━━━ site abandoned ━━━━

Freshwater mussel shell

III

━━━━ European artifacts ━━━━

ceramic style change
corn begins here
C R U S H E D   S H E L L

Freshwater snail shell

IV

━━━ pumpkin begins here ━━━

ceramic style change

Pleistocene sand

V

NOT EXCAVATED

2.16. Diagram of stratigraphy at Hontoon Island in 1988, showing natural and cultural changes.

If the observed strata in a specific unit are not an anomaly, the strata across the site can be tied together eventually (figs. 2.6 and 2.16).

In archaeology as in geology, the Law of Superposition is assumed; that is, layer after layer is deposited and not disturbed so that the youngest layers will be at the top and the oldest at the bottom. This logical arrangement can be affected by ancient or modern activities, animal burrows, earthquakes, volcanoes, etc. The stratigraphic profile may record these events, and the archaeologist should always be aware they might be present. Certain features might not be recognized during excavations but may be apparent in the profile. Intrusions from a younger habitation level to an older one might also be seen, such as trash pits or burials. Stratigraphic records are a very important part of archaeology.

Column Samples

No matter how well excavations and screening are designed, there are certain materials that cannot be sorted well in the field. This is particularly true of environmental information such as small twigs and seeds, tiny fish bones, etc.

2.17. Locations where column samples were cut from the wall of the trench at Hontoon Island, 1984 (bottom); close-up (top).

Even with the use of $\frac{1}{8}$-inch screen, some important data are lost through the mesh or cannot be recovered properly given the usual time constraints. After excavations have been completed in a unit, the walls are cleaned and column samples are cut by zone and 10-cm levels (or partial levels) within zones. Each volumetric segment is 15 cm x 15 cm or larger. These samples are returned to the laboratory and examined by various specialists (botanists, zooarchaeologists, soil scientists, etc.) using a series of geologic screens and flotation methods (fig. 2.17).

An archaeologist is responsible for backfilling excavation units and for leaving the site in as good condition as possible. All equipment, supplies, and materials must be transported back to the home institution. Equipment must be cleaned and put away. Long-term curation and maintenance of archaeological specimens and field notes must be provided. The biggest jobs are ahead: analysis, interpretation, and writing.

SUMMARY

Interpretations of the past are based on what has been found in the field. Yet most archaeological field reports contain a statement similar to the following: "Using standard archaeological procedures, the site . . ." The reader never learns just how good (or bad) the field techniques and recovery methods really were. There are exceptions, such as the excellent account of the McKeithen site by Kohler (1978) and the description of Groves Orange Midden by McGee and Wheeler (1994). Very different but effective methods, dictated by the field situation, were used in both cases and are described thoroughly.

All sites discovered during survey and all sites that are excavated must be recorded in the Florida Site File (FSF). The forms used to enter sites on the FSF are discussed and illustrated in chapter 6. An investigator must be professionally qualified to undertake an archaeological field project. A knowledge of what to look for is a prerequisite to successful site surveys and excavations. Qualifications include an understanding of archaeological objectives and field methods plus a commitment to analyze materials recovered and publish a full account of the results. Any excavator who does not fulfill these obligations is "committing an act of vandalism against a natural [cultural] resource of ultimate public interest" (Heizer 1966:15).

THREE

 **ANALYSIS**

Archaeology began to develop as a profession around 1850. Approximately 100 years of this time was spent classifying artifacts and speculating about the people who made them. Speculation reached a new level in the mid-twentieth century when archaeologists attempted to test models based on the archaeological record before drawing conclusions about human behavior. Obviously, this approach could only be successful if the archaeological record was fairly complete and if individuals had a good grasp of what they were testing. It turns out that a great deal of analysis had never been attempted because questions had never been asked.

Materials and sites can be examined in a number of ways. In the beginning the shape and design of stone and ceramic artifacts were described, but virtually nothing was done with plant and animal remains except (sometimes) to record their presence. The purpose of this chapter is to discuss various animal, vegetable, and mineral components of archaeological sites—flora, fauna, stone, pottery, shell, and metals—and describe how they can be analyzed to increase our knowledge of past human activities. Art, architecture, insects, soils, climate, hydrology, geology, and endless other phenomena are studied when applicable.

The study of plants that survive at archaeological sites is called paleoethno-botany (sometimes archaeobotany). Paleoethnobotanists are able to recon-struct environments of the past and determine what plants were selected from those environments by human groups to make life physically and mentally comfortable.

If an archaeological site has been excavated in a controlled manner and its contents collected from fine-mesh screens and column samples to prevent the loss of small seeds and other plant parts, the paleoethnobotanist can detect:

1 The cultural evolution of resource utilization in a given environment; that is, those things that became important through time and those that were not available or were not collected because they were not **cost-effective**.

2 Ecological or climatic changes that necessitated modifications in the way resources were exploited.

3 The season(s) that a site was occupied.

4 The caloric and nutritional value of the foods collected. After all, if more calories are burned up than consumed, the collecting effort would not be very productive. On the other hand, not all plants were used for food.

5 When and if a culture changed from a hunting-gathering way of life to a society with a growing dependence on cultivated crops.

6 The presence of nonnative plants obtained either through trade or as a result of disruptions brought about by invasion, such as the events that followed the Columbian voyages. Orange or watermelon seeds, for example, set an age limit on sites in the Western Hemisphere because they could not have appeared until after A.D. 1492.

7 Changes in plant communities after a site has been abandoned. The vegeta-tion probably will not return entirely to its original composition. For in-stance, the gumbo limbo tree grows on deserted shell middens on Florida's Gulf coast.

A fraction of the samples collected in small-mesh screens are processed and the contents of this subsample are identified through a binocular microscope; type collections are used for comparison. Because of differential preservation, the paleoethnobotanist is usually unable to furnish a completely accurate pic-ture of how ancient human groups utilized plants or of the relative impor-tance of any particular species. For instance, nut shells, fruit pits, and corn cobs survive because those plant parts are not consumed, whereas starchy roots are archaeologically invisible even though historic accounts mention that they formed an important part of the aboriginal diet.

In addition to food, plants or plant parts were used for medicines, rituals, dyes, cordage, weapons, utensils, canoes, building materials, firewood, and more. Leaves, stems, fibers, and even fungi were utilized. The leaves of *Ilex vomitoria,* for example, were brewed to make the black drink, but documentation for this practice is found only in written accounts or is implied by the recovery of shell cups from archaeological sites. In Florida, the archaeological record is biased toward the survival of carbonized remains unless the materials have been continuously waterlogged (fig. 3.1).

While water-saturated sites provide the best opportunity in Florida to recover representative samples of environmental and cultural "trash," many species may not survive under even these optimal conditions. By referring to historic records or by studying modern ecological situations, the paleoethnobotanist is often able to flesh out the record and determine what is missing.

A

B

3.1. (a) A portion of the gourd and pumpkin seeds recovered from a single 10-cm level of a 1-meter waterlogged square at Hontoon Island in 1988; (b) the preservation in waterlogged deposits is excellent, making it possible to identify differences in related plants such as the gourd and pumpkin varieties shown here.

3.2. (a) Prehistoric canoe made of pine recovered from a peat deposit on Ollie Stricklin's property, Clay County, Florida; (b) the same canoe two years later, after its holding pond dried out.

The ultimate goals are to "create a model of the environment in which a culture operated, the plant exploitation strategies pursued within that environment" and to assess the "stability and longevity of subsistence practices" (Scarry 1985:181). A **catchment area** within a few kilometers of a site is considered the limits of the economic potential of plant resources from a particular habitat because collecting from a greater distance would not be cost-effective. Of course, canoe travel would increase the catchment area. Most analyses have revealed that people used nearby resources when they were available and abundant. I hasten to add that the native peoples of Florida were not aware that modern-day economic theory would be applied to interpret their foraging activities.

Certain wood species were selected for their properties. Pine was used for creating large carvings. Pine and occasionally cypress were used to manufacture canoes (fig. 3.2). Double-ended pestles were made almost exclusively of lignum vitae for thousands of years, although a double-ended pestle made of oak was recovered at the 7,000–8,000-year-old Windover site. Other examples of selectivity probably can be found, but in most cases wood utilization seems to have corresponded to availability. At Hontoon Island, for example, five

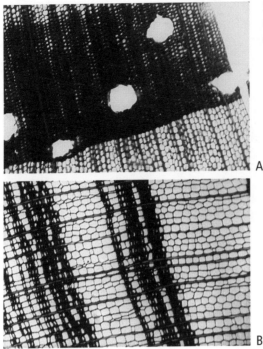

3.3. Microscopic cross-sections of (a) pine, showing resin canals; (b) cypress.

A

B

different species (cypress, pine, elm, ash, and bay) had been shaped into posts. Nevertheless, the woods are a key to habitats exploited.

The identification of wood species is complex and requires specialized training. Radial, cross, and tangential thin sections are prepared, examined under a microscope, and compared to type collections (fig. 3.3). The wood anatomist soon recognizes commonly occurring species or those having commercial value. Certain woods, like tropical or subtropical species, for which no taxonomic keys are available, present a real challenge.

Palynology, or **pollen** analysis, is often used to identify plants that have not survived or to confirm the findings of other analyses. A continuous 50,000-year climatic sequence has been documented based on the pollen record recovered in cores taken from several deep lakes in Florida.

In reality, it is difficult to determine unquestionably whether or not most plants recovered from archaeological contexts were actually utilized by human groups or were deposited from the natural vegetation in the surrounding area. Newsom (1987) furnishes an excellent discussion of the problem. There are three fairly sure ways to recognize if humans were involved in the manipulation of plants:

1 If coprolites (fecal material) have survived, their contents furnish unequivocal evidence that certain species were consumed.
2 If cultivated species, such as corn, are present.
3 If plants are recovered that are not native to a habitat within the catchment
   area.

Exciting new genetic studies using DNA (deoxyribonucleic acid), the substance stored in cell nuclei that copies hereditary patterns when cells are reproduced, are beginning to unravel relationships among plant species. This
information would be of great interest, for instance, in determining the origins and changes in squash and corn varieties as they spread throughout the
Americas in Precolumbian times.

FAUNA

The study of animal remains from archaeological sites is called *zooarchaeology*.
Paleontology is a term used for the investigation of ancient or fossil animals. If
an archaeologist anticipates that faunal specimens will be found during excavations, plans for their recovery and analysis should be made before the field
project begins to allow the zooarchaeologist to interpret correctly the importance of the animals to the people who used them. The zooarchaeologist can
detect:

1 Animal species present.
2 The minimum number of individuals (MNI) of each species.
3 Changes through time in the species utilized and/or those that were present
   in the area whether or not utilized by human groups; for instance, some
   animals are an indicator of climatic change.
4 Amount of meat contributed to the diet by the remains being analyzed.
5 The season(s) of the year the site was occupied based on the animal species
   recovered.
6 The habitats of the animals represented, i.e., marine, freshwater, terrestrial,
   etc.
7 The extent of the catchment area involved, i.e., how far the inhabitants had
   to travel to obtain the animals.
8 The kinds of procurement techniques utilized, i.e., gathering as with shellfish, nets, hook and line, traps, spears, etc., and whether boats were necessary.
9 Nonsubsistence use of animals.

All of the above determinations impose a responsibility on the archaeologist to excavate systematically, to use screens with mesh size small enough to assure the collection of bones from very small animals, and to provide the zooarchaeologist a sample large enough to be statistically valid. Diversity is a function of sample size, and 200 individuals is considered the minimum number needed to assure that most species are represented.

If possible the zooarchaeologist will identify the bone to **species** and body part. A good comparative collection containing all ages and both sexes of each taxon is crucial. Complete bones are needed for some identifications but in other cases, such as teeth, only a fragment is required. Some animals contribute more identifiable remains to the archaeological record than others. For instance, young animals may be underrepresented in deposits because their bones are not as dense as older animals and this may affect survival. In addition, larger animals tend to be noted more often than smaller ones because of biases introduced as a result of recovery methods, identification techniques, and quantification procedures. Some important species might not be identified at all. If, for instance, sardines are eaten whole, their remains would be found only in coprolites, which may not be present in the same deposits as food remains.

The minimum number of individuals of any one animal species is determined by using the principle of paired elements. Paired elements simply means the same-side bone in a bilaterally symmetrical animal. For instance, if two ulna bones from the left foreleg of a deer are recovered at a site, it is safe to conclude that the minimum number of deer present is two. It might be possible to say that three deer were present if the two left ulnae differ significantly in size from a right ulna recovered, suggesting that the right ulna came from an animal of different size or age. Some elements cannot be paired, such as scales, vertebrae, and carapace (turtle or tortoise shell) fragments. As a result, the MNI is probably underrepresented when nonpaired elements are used for identification.

A major goal of both archaeologist and zooarchaeologist is to determine how the bones present in a deposit contributed to the diet and nutrition of the people who put them there. This is not an easy task and requires that a skeletal weight or a skeletal dimension to body weight formula be used to estimate total body mass (biomass) in order to calculate the relationship between body weight and usable meat weight. The basic principle involved is that the proportion of skeletal mass to body mass changes with size. The assumption is that "bones are inedible residues of animals whose flesh was eaten"

(Wing and Loucks 1985). Since the recovery of a few elements does not necessarily mean that an entire animal was consumed, analysis should contain the meat weight for only those bones present (fig. 3.4a).

There is no single formula sufficient to make comparisons of the dietary importance of different fauna because the ratio of bone weight:body weight: meat weight differs with the various classes of animals. For example, 95 percent of the total body weight of fish is meat compared to 65 percent for mammals, 60 percent for turtles, and 50 percent for crabs and lobsters. An estimate

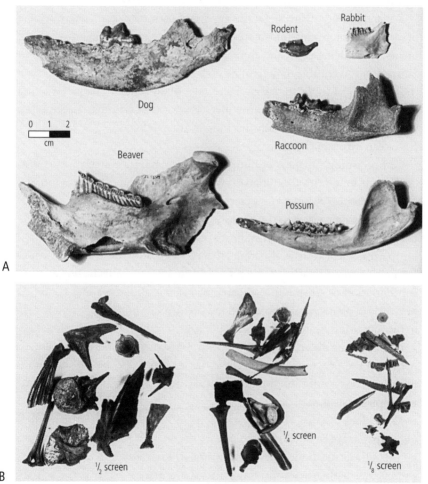

3.4. (a) Jaws of a variety of animals recovered in excellent condition from the water-saturated deposits at Groves Orange Midden, Volusia County, Florida; (b) fish vertebra and other bones from Hontoon Island, showing size variations from $^1/_2$, $^1/_4$, and $^1/_8$-inch mesh screens.

of available meat from fish is calculated by measuring the diameter of verte-brae. A 2-mm vertebra centrum equals $\frac{1}{4}$ pound of usable meat (fig. 3.4b).

There is, in addition, a lack of correspondence between the number of in-dividuals recovered and their biomass. For instance, one calculation showed that a single carcass of a red deer was the equivalent in calories to 52,267 oys-ters (Renfrew and Bahn 1991:259). Many small fish may not have a combined biomass as great as one large shark (Wing and Loucks 1985). On the other hand, capturing one shark may have been more calorie consuming and less certain than netting a dozen fish (Reitz and Scarry 1985).

Zooarchaeological investigations applied to early contact sites have resulted in some very interesting information that is seldom recorded in historic docu-ments. In studying plant and animal remains from St. Augustine, Reitz and Scarry (1985) were able to determine how much the Spanish depended upon their traditional foods for survival and how many kinds of native American foods were incorporated into the diet. They found also that acculturation went in both directions, with the Indians quickly adopting some available European subsistence items.

Carbon isotope analysis of human bone collagen can often reveal a great deal about long-term food intake—we are what we eat. Differing ratios of carbon isotopes ^{13}C and ^{12}C, determined by mass spectrometry, can show whether the diet was based primarily on land or marine plants and on $C3$ plants (temperate grasses, trees, shrubs) or $C4$ plants (tropical grasses includ-ing maize). Scientists have also found that concentrations of strontium, a stable mineral component of bone, can provide data on diet. Bones having a greater concentration of strontium compared to calcium indicate a diet composed primarily of plants, while those with lower concentrations suggest more meat in the diet. Modifications in these patterns are useful in determining changes in diet or status differences in food consumption; for example, the elite ate meat and the peasants did not. These methods provide additional ways to help the archaeologist interpret the relative importance of plants and animals to people in the past.

Most of the discussion in the paragraphs above has been based on method-ology that has been developed to enhance the recovery, analysis, and interpre-tation of the actual bone remains from archaeological sites. The archaeologist and zooarchaeologist are also concerned about more subjective issues. These include such questions as, how did the bone enter the site and how has it been altered since it was first deposited? How did human and nonhuman factors modify samples before, during, and after deposition? For instance, if animals are slaughtered elsewhere, could one expect that only certain portions of their skeleton will be recovered? Did food preparation methods have an effect on what remains? If there is an abrupt change in the composition of a deposit from one level to the next, does it mean that there were drastic cultural changes or merely an alteration in disposal patterns? How much disturbance to the deposit was caused by burrowing animals, rise and fall of the water table, or freezing and thawing? While these are all legitimate questions and certainly should be addressed, concrete conclusions must be based on what is actually found in the archaeological record. The assessment of what has happened to a bone between its deposition and its discovery is called **taphonomy**.

Another question that is not always easy to answer is, what criteria can be used to establish whether or not an animal was utilized or is present because it was part of the natural environment? The answer is easy if bones have been butchered or modified into artifacts. In other cases, the solution is not so clear, particularly if some of the questionable remains are from animals that we would not dream of eating today although they may have been consumed in the past. This kind of **ethnocentrism** biases our interpretation of the archaeological record.

Another aspect of faunal analysis is experimentation to determine how bone weapons, implements, ornaments, beads, etc., were manufactured, decorated, and used. It is a time-consuming and difficult task to cut, shape, and incise bone using stone, shell, sharks teeth, and other natural products. These kinds of investigations provide important insights about human behavior and values.

STONE

Certain areas of Florida have stone outcrops containing chert material suitable for the manufacture of chipped stone implements. The outcrops occur primarily in the central highland region and the Tampa embayment. By the time native people first entered Florida, they could recognize quality chert and the kinds of geologic deposits where it could be found. In other words, they knew where to look for and quarry it. After all, humans had been using and experimenting with stone for about 2 million years, long before they entered the Western Hemisphere.

The study of stone remains from archaeological sites is called **lithic technology**. This term is extended to include experiments that replicate styles and use wear.

By examining stone remains, the archaeologist and lithic technologist can usually:

1 Interpret their function.
2 Estimate the age of implements either by their style, by their stratigraphic position in the deposit, or through sophisticated dating techniques.
3 Determine the kinds of stone the implements were made from and their composition.
4 Describe how they were made.

The first question asked when someone finds a spearhead is, how old is it? At present, there is no available technique in Florida that can furnish a date for archaeological stone remains falling within the time frame that the major human occupations occurred here, about 10,000+ years. (See discussion of thermoluminescence in chapter 4.) Therefore, the age of a stone artifact must be based on radiocarbon analysis of associated organic materials or on the comparative method, i.e., styles and attributes similar to those securely dated elsewhere. The stratigraphic position of a stone implement in a deposit might provide a relative age (younger/older depending on depth) but not an absolute date. Despite these problems, a sequence of major stone artifact styles has been established for Florida. **Classification**, or typology, is the mechanism that permits the recognition of specific artifacts and their approximate antiquity.

Stone tools, particularly sophisticated spearheads, are end products of processes of manufacture utilizing numerous techniques. They are also end products of a technology that took hundreds of thousands of years to develop. Ancient flint**knappers** could recognize good quality stone material; they knew where to find it and how to flake it into tools. This knowledge is not so apparent to archaeologists. The ability to produce implements from flint was lost in the Old World, except in isolated areas, when metals (particularly iron) were substituted for stone several millennia ago.

By studying stone debris from chert (flint) quarry sites, it is possible to reconstruct the steps involved in producing weapons or implements, including the initial procurement and fracture of large chert boulders (fig. 3.5a). Chert has a fracture pattern similar to non**crystalline** glass (fig. 3.5b) because of its randomly oriented microcrystalline structure of silica dioxide. When chert is struck in a controlled manner with the correct force and angle, a predictable flake can be removed. An experienced flintknapper could remove flake after flake until the desired tool was completed. In the case of spearhead manu-

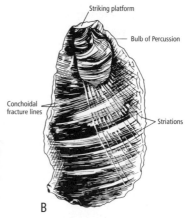

Striking platform

Bulb of Percussion

Conchoidal
fracture lines

Striations

B

3.5. (a) The author attempting to
fracture a large chert boulder using the
block-on-block technique; (b) a stone
flake showing typical fracture
characteristics of noncrystalline and
microcrystalline rock.

A

facture, symmetry in shape, thickness, and flake size was maintained throughout the production process. But accidents did happen and even the most talented craftsman occasionally misplaced a blow or encountered a hidden fossil, and the specimen broke. Quarry sites were visited for thousands of years
and contain thousands of failures. Since these failures occurred at various stages
of manufacture, they provide clues to the step-by-step processes involved in
making tools from the very first flake removed from a chert boulder to the
final **pressure flake**.

For some implements the process of manufacture included heating (thermal alteration) of the stone material to make it easier to flake, sharper, and
more beautiful. This technology began in Florida about 9,000 years ago and
continued to historic contact in the sixteenth century. To accomplish thermal
alteration successfully, the material was first chipped into its approximate final form using a method called **direct percussion**. It was then embedded in
sand, underlain and overlain with hot coals, gradually heated to around 350°C
(for Florida chert), and cooled slowly. Direct exposure to fire or rapid heating
and cooling results in crazing, **potlidding**, or explosion of the material, ren-
dering it useless.

Thermal alteration reduces the point tensile strength of Florida chert by 50 percent, thus allowing the craftsman to better control the removal of flakes using both percussion and pressure and produce a thinner and sharper product. The chert becomes sharper and more glasslike when reflaked after heating because the **microcrystals** that make up the structure of the stone are fused when the elements comprising the intercrystalline spaces reach the melting point (**eutectic development**). The technique was applied primarily to spearheads because they function better if they are thinner, sharper, and very symmetrical. A more subjective interpretation might be that their color (usually pink or red) and luster, compared to nonheated chert, appealed to the hunter, who may have believed these qualities would attract the animal he was seeking to kill (see figs. 1.13 and 1.14). This explanation moves us into the realm of ritual and belief systems. Spearheads were not merely tools to make a tool (like a hammer) but objects used to accomplish a task (provide meat). Thermal alteration would not have been practical where strength was needed (as for a hammer) because the material becomes too brittle and shatters easily.

Thermal alteration usually can be detected on stone remains even after thousands of years because of their vitreous luster and pinkish-reddish cast. The color is due to the presence of iron, which causes the natural beige-brown rock to change to pink-red when heated (Purdy and Brooks 1971).

There are times when it is revealing to determine the elemental composition of flint materials. By establishing standards or fingerprints for Florida cherts, it should be possible to identify non-Florida materials if one suspects that such specimens have been recovered at a site. Tests are expensive, time consuming, and require sophisticated instrumentation as well as the skills of highly trained individuals. In other words, the results must be worth the effort. I have used neutron activation analysis (NAA), proton-induced X-ray emission analysis (PIXE), and X-ray diffraction analysis with success to identify elements and trace elements in quantities of parts per million (PPM) or parts per billion (PPB).

An easier way to identify the geographic sources of chert materials might be through their fossils. Florida cherts are all replaced limestones of the Cenozoic era and contain fossils typical of the various epochs within the Cenozoic, i.e., Eocene, Oligocene, and Miocene. Flint materials from many of the other states in the Southeast, except coastal areas, would have fossils common to the Paleozoic or Mesozoic eras. Color, texture, and other attributes are not reliable source indicators, even though an individual familiar with local sources

3.6. Stone artifacts from the Suwannee River. The flake scars have disappeared from their surfaces as a result of water moving over them for a long time.

might suspect that certain specimens are from out of state based on their "look."

Florida has no plutonic or volcanic rock, so if artifacts manufactured from these materials are found they must have been imported. Also, a few objects made of steatite (soapstone), a non-Florida material, entered the state by at least 6,000 years ago.

The composition and physical appearance of chert materials can be altered by chemical and mechanical weathering processes. Water and/or wind can obliterate flake scars from a chipped stone tool so thoroughly that it is sometimes difficult to determine if the object was modified by humans (fig. 3.6). In other cases, the surface of an artifact has become roughened (and flake scars may disappear) when there is a breakdown of the silica bonds (known as static weathering). As with mechanical weathering, it cannot be concluded that these specimens are artifacts unless they have retained a recognizable shape.

Another kind of weathering phenomenon may have potential use as a dating technique. This is called patina formation, in which, through a diffusion process, there is selective leaching of elements (primarily iron) from the chert surface (known as dynamic weathering). The **patinated** or surface weathered layer is nearly white in contrast to the brown or gray interior (fig. 3.7). If the rate of patina formation could be calculated it should be possible to deter-

3.7. Chert specimen from the Container Corporation of America site, Marion County, Florida. The specimen has been sawed in half to reveal in cross-section the weathering rind (patina) that developed after thousands of years.

0   1   2
cm

mine the age of stone implements. But even though weathering always takes time, it can occur rapidly or slowly depending upon environmental conditions and the composition of the chert material. In order for patina formation to be used as a dating technique, therefore, it would be necessary to establish a reaction formula for each site and it would require large numbers of specimens and precise control over excavation procedures.

Another type of weathering is the development of rock varnish that forms over petroglyphs and surface artifacts in the southwestern United States. Efforts to calibrate the age of rock varnish in order to obtain a date for the artifact or petroglyph underlying it have been fairly successful. Minerals that accumulate on Florida artifacts might be dated in a similar manner but no investigations have been conducted.

Experiments to replicate stone tool types have been carried out for generations. By reproducing stone tools, archaeologists gain insights into the problems faced by aboriginal flintknappers. These studies accelerated in the 1960s with the work of Francois Bordes and Don Crabtree and continue to this day. Replicative experiments were extended to investigations of use wear. Macroscopic and microscopic examination of use wear on stone scrapers, knives, and hammers indicated that specific types of damage occurred on implements depending on how they functioned and the material with which they came in contact, i.e., hardwood, softwood, bone, etc. Experiments to reproduce use wear and analysis of the results have broadened the interpretative potential of stone remains from archaeological sites.

CERAMICS

The controlled heating of clay to temperatures high enough to induce irreversible changes in its chemical structure is one of the great achievements of humankind. Clay is the most versatile of all substances that are altered through pyrotechniques. Not only do different temperatures affect the final product but it is possible to decorate the plastic raw material and shape it into infinite sizes and forms, thus creating a bonanza for archaeological interpretation. Until recently, this aspect of ceramic technology has been the focus of most studies of ceramic remains from archaeological sites.

As early as 26,000 years ago in several locations in Europe, clays were shaped into figurines and then fired; yet the general use of pottery vessels did not occur for another 15 millennia in the Old World and not until 5000 B.P. in the Western Hemisphere. Almost immediately, pottery objects became culturally and chronologically specific, so that today archaeologists can recognize the spatial and temporal origins of literally hundreds of ceramic designs and forms. This knowledge is especially valuable in the absence of stratigraphic control and when no **absolute dating** method can be utilized.

The ceramic technologist is able to determine:

1 The composition of the clay materials and if they came from a source close to the archaeological site where the pottery vessels or sherds were found.
2 What was included as **temper**.
3 The firing temperature.
4 If the methods of producing ceramic pieces were uniform, suggesting specialization, or if there was a lack of uniformity, suggesting that pottery making was a nonspecialized craft.

As mentioned in chapter 1, Florida archaeologists have used pottery vessels and sherds for generations to establish regional and temporal differences based particularly on decoration but also, to a certain extent, on temper. Tempers, or **aplastics**, are inclusions added to the clay that strengthen it and decrease the chance of shrinking or cracking during firing. Temper often also refers to the aplastics that may have been naturally present in clays. Orange period pottery was tempered with fiber; Deptford and most South Florida pottery was sand-tempered; and St. Johns Ware was tempered with sponge spicules. Sherd, limestone, and other tempering products have been noted. But questions remained unanswered because precise analysis of all components of the fired piece had not been conducted nor had there been attempts to identify clay sources.

The pioneering work of Shepard (1976) stimulated research in Florida that has gone a long way to solve enduring problems of Florida prehistory. Elemental composition of clay materials, tempers, particle sizes, firing temperatures, hardness, thickness, etc., have been quantified and standardized through microscopic studies (including scanning electron microscopy) and experimentation. These tests have revealed differences in pastes that cannot be detected macroscopically. The following examples demonstrate how these kinds of investigations can verify, refute, or clarify long-held beliefs and enigmas pertaining to the prehistoric ceramic industry in Florida.

One long-held belief is that most ceremonial Weeden Island pottery was not produced locally. Trace element and cluster analyses, however, have demonstrated that several local as well as nonlocal clay sources were used to manufacture effigy and other Weeden Island series pottery recovered at the McKeithen site. It now seems that a multicenter model is more appropriate for the manufacture of Weeden Island ceremonial pottery. The broader implication of these investigations is that a sacred-secular model for this pottery is too simplistic: "While certain pottery types do occur more frequently in mound or sacred contexts, as do certain vessel forms, differences in terms of methods and materials of manufacture are based on decoration, and not on depositional context" (Cordell 1984:197). Cordell was also able to support the belief that specialization will be evident or most easily recognized in elite ceramics because of greater standardization of paste composition and greater skill in manufacture and firing. In other words, while each household probably made its own utilitarian items, special purpose pottery for ritual was probably not produced by everyone.

Another frustrating and seemingly unsolvable ceramic problem has been attacked successfully. From as early as 500 B.C. to as late as the time of European contact in the sixteenth century, the most abundant pottery of Southwest Florida consisted of an undecorated, sandy-textured ware commonly referred to as Glades Plain, or simply Sand-tempered Plain. The longevity and apparent homogeneity of this plain pottery limited its role as a chronological tool. But this situation is probably due more to the lack of systematic quantification and standardization of differences than to the absence of such differences. Some chronological changes in Sand-tempered Plain pottery have been noted by archaeologists, such as vessel and rim form, hardness, thickness, and paste, but no rigorous analytical techniques were applied to determine the reality of these observed trends. The understanding of variability in Southwest Florida ceramics has now been improved by the analysis of physical, mineralogical, technological, and formal properties of the pottery. There are considerable differences in pastes, clay sources, tempers, firing temperatures, consistency in manufacture, etc. Some of these attributes may have chronological significance.

The application of similar types of analytical procedures detected paste and technological variability in a sample of Deptford (500 B.C.–A.D. 800) and Savannah (A.D. 800–1500) pottery sherds from the St. Marys region. The results indicate that the data may be useful in predicting the temporal affiliation of pottery assemblages that lack a clear-cut distinction in surface treatment or in the absence of diagnostic decorated types or other datable remains. In this case, three gross paste categories were identified representing 10 to 15 clay sources. It was demonstrated that Deptford and Savannah period pottery can be distinguished in terms of paste as well as surface treatment.

Analytical techniques used to study pottery remains need to be standardized. Very often descriptions and measurements of such attributes as aplastics, particle sizes, etc., are undefined or vaguely defined, making it impossible to use data comparatively. In the study of Deptford and Savannah sherds, for example, magnification of 105x was necessary to detect the presence of sponge spicules in the paste. Obviously, if the material had been examined with a hand lens or any other form of lower magnification, this important distinguishing constituent would have been missed. A remaining problem is the need to identify clay sources. It is one thing to recognize that pottery clays come from different sources, but clays may have been altered by additions (aplastics) or subtractions so the source cannot be easily matched with the pottery.

Clues to foods eaten or pigments used can be identified sometimes by residues remaining in pots. Thermoluminescence could possibly date ceramic remains successfully, but this method has not been used extensively in Florida (see chapter 4).

In summary, a new material is created because of chemical changes that occur when clays are fired. Fired clay remains are practically indestructible, even though sometimes the original forms have been broken into dozens of fragments called sherds. In Florida, pottery has been the most important material used to understand cultural variability through time and space. The recovery of "exotic" sherds from archaeological sites confirms the existence of cultural contacts with other groups.

Freshwater and marine shellfish species became important food items in Florida by 6000 B.P. Marine shell, in addition, furnished a source of raw material for all manner of tools, utensils, and ornaments. Some bone and shell artifacts substituted for stone in areas where stone was not available, such as along the entire East coast, the Gulf Coast south of the Tampa embayment, and all of South Florida. Several artifact types (e.g., celts, beads, pendants) abundant in shell were never produced from local chert; such types, manufactured from imported (polished) stone, are occasionally recovered from archaeological sites in Florida. Stoneworking, in general, except for spearheads and, later on, arrowheads, declined after shell technology was developed.

Shell analysis includes:

1 Identification of species.
2 Whether or not the animal was used as food.
3 Seasonality.
4 Methods used to modify shell including replicative and usewear studies.
5 Types and functions of shell tools, utensils, and ornaments.
6 Social implications.

Numerous varieties of marine gastropods and pelecypods were available in greater or lesser abundance to the Indians of Florida. Gastropods recovered at archaeological sites include species of *Busycon* and *Strombus* (commonly called whelks or conchs) and *Oliva*. Pelecypods (bivalves) include *Crassostrea virginica* (oysters), the heavy-bodied *Mercenaria campechiensis* (quahogs), and many other less robust types. Marine shellfish are fairly easy to gather and contain generous portions (as much as two pounds in some conchs) of delicious, edible meat. The assumption is that most of these animals were used for food and then the shells of some of them were made into implements or decorative items. An exception may be the deepwater *Arca*, which probably was not procured by the Indians, but whose shells, which washed up on the beach, were used as sinkers or scrapers. Many researchers have inferred that a hole in the large conchs indicates that they were struck a blow to break the columnar muscle attachment to remove the animal. Reiger (1979, 1981) makes three excellent comments in this regard: (1) the blow would have to be directed to a very specific location above the shoulder, (2) there are no holes in the majority of nonartifactual conch shells, and (3) it would be more sensible to keep the animals wet and alive until they were transported to their final destination and then kill them by exposing them to fire or steam, permitting the easy extraction of the meat.

It is a tedious task to examine the contents of the massive shell middens along the coastline of Florida and segregate artifacts from food debris or use as construction materials (fig. 3.8). In contrast, when marine shells are recovered from freshwater shell middens, there is little question that these objects were imported and utilized; otherwise they would not be there. In order to determine the extent of modification that has occurred, it is absolutely essential that the analyst be familiar with the morphology of the living animal. What means were employed to cut, grind, drill, or incise these thick-walled species in order to produce the multitude of different styles? Very few ethnographic accounts exist that provide insights about the skills needed by the Indians to convert the gastropod and bivalve species into various artifact types, and only limited replicative studies have been conducted. Cushing (1897) seems to be the first person to pioneer such investigations in Florida. Because of the

3.8. Southwest Florida shell midden.

excellent preservation at Key Marco, Cushing was able to recover shell implements that retained lashings and handles in their original relation to one another.

> Picks, hammers, adzes, and gouges made from almost entire conch shells were found, handles and all, in relatively perfect condition. . . . The whorl was usually battered away on the side toward the mouth so as to expose the columella. The lip was roundly notched or pierced, and the back whorl also perforated oppositely. Thus the stick or handle could be driven into these perforations, past the columella in such manner that it was sprung or clamped firmly into place. Nevertheless it was usually further secured with rawhide thongs—now mere jelly—passed through one or two additional perforations in the head, and around both the stick and the columella. . . . I made a tool of this description [a gouge], which worked admirably on the hardest wood I could get; and retained its edge amazingly well. (Cushing 1897:368)

Lashings made from plant fibers had survived in excellent condition. Cushing also experimented with making and using other shell tools. His observations and conclusions have been modified somewhat through the years, but they form the base of all modern efforts to describe the production and function of marine shell objects.

Several researchers have replicated and used shell implements and ornaments from Florida recording, in some cases, the difficulty and time involved in manufacture and the wear patterns resulting from use.

Webster (1970) recovered shell vessels manufactured from *B. contrarium* in a Preceramic midden deposit near Astor. The vessels were burned on their bases and sides, and Webster concluded they had functioned as cooking utensils before pottery vessels were available. He identified similar specimens from other sites in the collections of the Florida Museum of Natural History at Gainesville. He then obtained a live *B. contrarium,* removed the animal, and chiseled the columella away to produce a vessel similar to the ones found at the sites:

> Water was boiled in this vessel over an open fire until approximately five gallons was evaporated. There was no noticeable damage except discoloration. Its properties as a cooking container are not unlike a modern type of ceramic cooking vessel. This shell's width is 10 cm and its capacity is one measured cup. The only observable disadvantage of the Busycon vessel as compared to a pottery vessel is its limited size. They do have a natural built in handle—the shell's siphonal canal. (Webster 1970:4)

Reiger (1979) concluded that the examination of unfinished implements furnish insights about processes of manufacture that cannot be detected by studying their end products. He compared the partially worked hole in a *Busycon* found by himself to one illustrated by Moore (1921) and deduced that the aperture to receive the haft was made by pecking rather than by drilling. The ragged edges were then rounded and smoothed with an abrader. According to Moore (1921), the implement he found was abandoned during manufacture of the hole because a crack had developed in the wall of the shell.

A second type of uncompleted shell tools reported by Reiger were conchs representing various stages in a technique for the controlled removal of all or part of the whorls of large marine gastropods. "After pecking out the holes, the Indians connected them by breaking out the spaces between them.... The method ... is analogous to creasing a sheet of paper to control how it separates when the paper is torn into two sections" (Reiger 1979:132, 134). Reiger, however, was left with the question of what kind of tool the Indians intended to make. He purchased six *Strombus gigas* and attempted to duplicate the archaeological specimens. Beginning at the lip, he used a heavy aboriginal shell celt to break away the whorl, punched holes in the inner whorl using a screwdriver and hammer, connected the holes, and broke out the columella. He concluded that only by making the holes in a fairly straight line would the break also occur in a straight line. He discovered that some of his columellae, formerly thought to be debitage, were actually tools. Thus, as a result of his replicative experiments, Reiger (1979:136, 137) proposed a new shell tool type for Florida.

Prentice (1983) used only aboriginal implements in an exhaustive (and exhausting) monumental experiment of shell tool replication. He made his own flint tools to cut a knobbed whelk (*Busycon carica* [Gmelin]) in order to manufacture a shell cup. After 386 minutes (nearly 6½ hours), wearing out 60 flint flakes in the process, Prentice was able to detach a large triangular section from the body of the shell (fig. 3.9a). While this method consumes considerably more time, energy, and flint than does bashing, it is more accurate and aesthetically pleasing and it conserves the shell. Prentice (1983) also conducted experiments on the same whelk to determine the length of time and amount of flint needed to remove the columella and to cut small sections in order to produce beads. "After 1391 minutes (slightly more than 23 hours) of cutting time and the use of 191 flakes, the *Busycon* had been reduced to one cup, three columella pieces, and 17 bead blanks" (Prentice 1983). He then proceeded to drill holes in the bead blanks (averaging about 20 minutes each; fig. 3.9b)

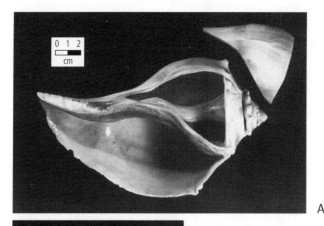

A

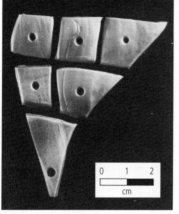

B

3.9. (a) Triangular piece cut from the body of a large whelk after 6$\frac{1}{2}$ hours of effort; (b) drilled bead blanks made from the same whelk.

with a flint microdrill and discovered that heat-altered blades produced from Florida chert were superior to unheated blades for drilling. "After the holes are drilled, the blanks are strung on a line and run through a grooved sandstone abrader in order to make them round and uniform in size" (Prentice 1986, personal communication).

Another investigator conducted experiments to replicate *Strombus gigas* celts. The process involved removing the lip from the shell to produce a blank and modification of the blank to complete the celt. Percussion methods were used followed by grinding of the edges and bit into final form. Cutting with shark teeth or imported flint and grinding with sandstone or limerock may have been important manufacturing techniques used by the Indians. Attempts to reproduce use wear resulted in only small nicks, and it was concluded that shell is very durable and probably requires long-term utilization before impact breakage occurs or rejuvenation is necessary. Debitage from the Cheetum and Flagami sites in Dade County was studied to verify observations of the replicative experiments.

Moore (1900:380) says that "Florida may be called the home of the shell implements in this country, for no other State has such an extent of subtropical sea coast where shells abound, and in no other State is such a need created through absence of stone." Some authors believed the conchs were used as war clubs, and some of them may have been, but, as Moore points out, the conchs are too numerous to have all served that purpose. They were so abundant, in fact, that modern settlers had to remove them before they could plant crops.

Various species of marine shells were used for hammers; adzes; celts; gouges; picks; digging tools; awls; chisels; anvils; anchors; canoe bailers; vessels for drinking, cooking, and serving; spoons; weights or sinkers; knives; scrapers; smoothers; "spatulas"; gorgets; pendants; and beads (see examples in chapter 1). At Key Marco, Cushing found shell disks that were used as eyes for the wooden masks, shell ear buttons, and a bivalve with a painted figure (Gilliland 1975:169–204). Goggin (1949) created a typology for the multitude of shell artifacts that had been described in the literature since the nineteenth century. Goggin's classification has been used and modified through the years. Griffin describes the confusion as follows:

> Goggin's classification includes over 70 types or categories and attempts to cover the entire South Florida area. Willey ... in his Belle Glade and Dade-Broward report included only 31 types or varieties, not always matching Goggin's. Gilliland ... grouped the Key Marco shell artifacts into about 60 types or categories, again not completely matching Goggin's classification. To further confuse the issue, the analysis of the shell artifacts ... from the Granada site largely ignored previous work and established 33 object categories which are often difficult to match with any of the other systems. (Griffin 1988:80)

The problem exists because shell is so versatile and durable. There are probably very few pristine types, except perhaps decorative items. If energy had been expended to create an implement from a *Busycon* or *Strombus,* it might have functioned eventually for a variety of tasks and the original use wear would be modified or obliterated altogether. Several authors have addressed this situation. There is also the need to consider human variation, both with regard to the production of artifacts and the way in which they were utilized. A major lack, of course, is our ability to comprehend how these items were actually used. They may have functioned as hammers or scrapers, but what did they pound and scrape? The edge angle of a cutting tool and the way it was hafted may suggest that it was an axe or adze, but what purpose it served will always elude us unless entire tool kits are found together.

In Florida, Cushing's (1897) finds at Key Marco will forever be our most valuable clue. Present-day societies without stone or metal do not exist for observation, and descriptions from early historic accounts seldom furnish enough detail. The Indians needed shell in their fishing activities and to work wood, bone, and probably hides. Vessels and spoons were produced most commonly from *B. contrarium* because of its thinner body and probably also because of its availability. *Strombus gigas* was the best substitute for stone (Griffin 1988) and was preferred for making celts because of its heavy body, but celts were also made from various species of *Busycon*. Beads were made from *Oliva,* and beads, pendants, and gorgets were fashioned from columella and walls of *Busycon*. Shell pendants are very abundant; they are seldom engraved. The left valve of quahogs *(Mercenarium campechiensis* [Gmelin]), the largest heaviest bivalve shell in Florida, may have been selected differentially, suggesting some kind of cultural preference, e.g., handedness. The analyst must also be aware that shell scrap, resulting from the manufacture of formal shell tool types, could itself have been used expediently and should be examined. Another point is that some modifications noted on shell may not be the result of human activities. For instance, holes that look man-made may have been produced by marine predators; some damage to the lips of quahogs comes from *Busycon* predator attacks, and stone crabs, in turn, attack the whelks.

Shell is very abundant at South Florida sites. More than 95 percent of nonceramic artifacts are made of shell. Most of them come from only a few genera and can be classified into numerous fairly common types. Some of them are not that well made. After Willey (1949a) completed his examination of shell artifacts from Belle Glade and other sites, he concluded that they were the same varieties as found elsewhere. It appears that when actual counts are made, a few typical shell tools form the vast majority of those recovered. The great complexity that seems to exist may result because people are "splitters" instead of "lumpers" and from the classification of rare atypical specimens. Numerous similar artifacts from different locales are needed to create types and to assure that one is not describing interesting but nevertheless eccentric pieces.

With regard to chronology, observations have been made about differences between shell tool types and methods of manufacture at early shell-using sites dating to the Late Archaic and at more recent sites. Through time, the types become more varied and their production is more specialized and uniform.

Mention should be made of name changes for some of the marine shell species since the late nineteenth and early and middle twentieth centuries. *Pleuroploca gigantea* was formerly *Fasciolaria,* commonly called horse conch or triton. *Busycon* has replaced *Fulgar* as the genus name for conchs. *B. contrarium,* the left-handed whelk or lightning whelk, was formerly *B. perversa.*

Not all species are available in all locations. *S. gigas,* for example, is found on Florida's east coast but is rare on the west coast. Geographical, temporal, or seasonal availability should be taken into account when analysis is conducted on shell remains from archaeological sites. A technique was used to determine seasonal occupation patterns of southern quahogs *(Mercenaria campechiensis)* from Charlotte Harbor, Florida. Growth increments in the shells show them to be accurate recorders of the animal's life history and, like tree rings, they record environmental changes. Shell growth is associated with seasonal environmental cycles throughout the year. These data may be useful in estimating the time of quahog harvest, i.e., **seasonality studies** of site occupation by human groups. Since the growth patterns of *Mercenaria* are similar between adjacent months but are distinct for adjacent seasons, it should be possible to determine if they were harvested in the spring, summer, fall, or winter. These studies require considerable time and expertise; they are still in progress.

METAL

Metals are not native to Florida, but artifacts of copper and silver (rarely) have been recovered at some Florida sites dating as early as A.D. 200. Gold, silver, copper, brass, and iron of European origin appear after historic contact in the early sixteenth century.

Metal artifacts have been examined to determine:

1 Whether or not metal working preceded European contact.
2 The geographic source of the metal and its composition.
3 If metal artifacts were reworked from European objects or from metals native to the Americas.

Now, because of modern radiometric dating methods and other techniques, no one questions the fact that copper ornaments and implements were present in Precolumbian Florida. There was, however, considerable debate about this topic in the late nineteenth and early twentieth centuries. Thanks to C.B. Moore's thorough study of metal objects from mounds throughout the eastern United States, his submission of copper fragments for compositional analysis, and his comparison of the results of these analyses to native American and European copper sources, he was able to conclude that many of the metal artifacts found in the mounds were made prior to and without the influence of European technology.

Despite Moore's painstaking investigations, there were dissenters, particularly J.D. McGuire, who prompted Moore to reiterate his findings in summary form: "[I]t was shown by many analyses that much of the copper of the mounds, including sheet copper, was native copper, and much purer than copper which is recovered from ores by smelting and especially from the arsenical, sulphide ores of Europe, which, treated by the earlier smelting processes, produced a very impure article indeed" (Moore et al. 1903:27). According to Moore, native American copper is greater than 99.5 percent pure with traces of silver and iron. European copper is usually less than 99.0 percent copper with impurities of silver, iron, arsenic, antimony, nickel, cobalt, lead, and other materials. Lead is the important component because it is not found in American or in native European copper but was added in the smelting process in Europe.

In addition to his analytical evidence, Moore commented on the uneven thickness of Indian-worked copper as compared to what it would have been if it had originated from Europeans and on the lack of "soldering or brazing" used in production or on repaired pieces. He also notes that associated objects of known European manufacture (gold, iron, glass, glazed earthenware, bronze, pewter, etc.) are missing in the mounds, except sometimes superficially: "I may say that among the many scores of mounds I have demolished, I have met with a number of large mounds where copper, including sheet copper, associated only with objects purely aboriginal, lay from bottom to top, so that it would seem hardly fair to say that copper is usually met with near the surface of mounds" (Moore et al. 1903:29).

McGuire was not convinced, and his statement is probably in accord with the beliefs of many people of that time: "The technical skill necessary to produce such material is of no mean order, and we are not accustomed to place the primitive Floridian in the human family above the average in culture of the American Indian as he was first found by Europeans. Had there been a people producing such objects at the advent of the whites, can it be questioned that such a fact would have been referred to by early writers who have recorded everything with which they came in contact worthy of notice?" (Moore et al. 1903). McGuire dismissed the well-known drawings and descriptions of metal ornaments made by LeMoyne after the French had settled in Florida at Fort Caroline in the 1560s: "The American Indian ... learned in Florida in 1518, and subsequent to the destruction of the Narváez expedition, much of the use of metal; he learned more from the de Soto expedition in 1540" (Moore et al. 1903:36). McGuire ignored the results of compositional analyses conducted on dozens of copper samples.

Moore was angry. He offered to furnish copper from both situations and name an expert to analyze them "that this matter may be settled, if it is not settled already" (Moore et al. 1903:32). About his dissenters, Moore concludes: "These gentlemen continue a Parthian method in science, where one shoots off statements and then flees from a demonstration of facts; these gentlemen must be relegated to the class represented by the worthy old lady in the story who said she had what was a great deal better than evidence, and that was her own opinion" (Moore et al. 1903:xvi).

Most researchers of the time agreed with Moore and, of course, subsequent verification through stratigraphy, associated artifacts, and radiometric dating methods has furnished unequivocal proof that Moore was correct. We now know that copper was in use during the Archaic (Old Copper culture, 5000 B.P.), Hopewell (over 2000 years B.P.), and Mississippian (A.D. 1000) time periods.

In one case, Moore mentions a very close correspondence in chemical composition between a copper artifact from the Tick Island site in Florida and source material from Cuba. He was aware of many locations where copper might be obtained but he concluded that the majority of aboriginal copper objects had been manufactured from copper originating in the Lake Superior region. An important clue is the presence of silver in Lake Superior copper, which is often visible in flakes, seams, and streaks. Silver evidently does not exist visibly in native copper from other locations in North America. Lake Superior was probably the source of silver used to manufacture the few objects of that material found at sites in the eastern United States. More recent researchers have furthered Moore's investigations of trace elements in copper from the Great Lakes region plus the triangle area of Tennessee, Georgia, and North Carolina.

Moore and other investigators of the late nineteenth and early twentieth centuries mention metal artifacts of both Pre- and Postcolumbian origin from many sites in Florida: Shields mound, Grant mound, Tick Island, Mount

Royal, Crystal River, etc. In late-twentieth-century publications, the presence of metal artifacts has been reported from Fort Center; the Tatham, Ruth Smith, and Weeki Watchee mounds; Hontoon Island; and the Lake Jackson site. Metal artifacts from Precolumbian sites include pendants; beads; breast plates; panpipes; effigies; celts; axes; chisels; objects sheathed in copper such as buttons, earspools, and animal jaws; and more. As mentioned above, most Precolumbian metal artifacts were made from copper, but a few items of silver have been recovered and, farther north, beads have been found manufactured from meteoritic iron.

Moore (1894) discussed to a certain extent the methods used by Native Americans to work, consolidate, and repair metal objects. He commented that sheets can be beaten from native copper with the aid of annealing, that complicated designs can be reproduced with aboriginal tools, and that repairs can be made with rivets. Moore deduced that Precolumbian metalworking did not include smelting or casting.

While Moore's primary objective was to demonstrate that copper objects existed prior to European contact, Leader (1985, 1988) asked a different set of questions. He studied the metal artifacts found in Historic period deposits at Fort Center in an effort to determine if they had been produced by Florida aborigines, by other New World peoples (for example, European captives brought from Central or South America), or by Europeans. Shipwrecks were probably the source of the metal (gold, silver, and copper), and Sears (1982:59) concluded that it had been reworked by the Indians. Leader hypothesized that many of the techniques and tools needed to work bone, wood, shell, stone, and plant fibers can be applied to metal and that the application of existing technologies should be visible in the finished product and distinguishable from European technology (Leader 1985:4).

Using simple microscopy, xeroradiography, and replication, Leader concluded that, while a few of the metal objects from Fort Center were of European or South American origin and unaltered, the majority had been modified by the Florida Indians. Xeroradiography is a nondestructive method that produces an X-ray image clear enough to ascertain fabrication techniques, patterns of wear, and identification of tool marks (Leader 1985:11). Leader (1985:49) was able to determine that some of the famous spider tablets were made from cast silver sheet. Reshaping by the Indians distorted the original casting voids.

Xeroradiography shows density shifts and folds and is also useful in revealing cracks not visible to the naked eye that should be reported to conservators. Leader replicated beads, cast figures, and silver tablets using methods available to the Indians. He duplicated marks by using stone, bone, shell awls, and shark teeth. He demonstrated that shark teeth make excellent engraving tools. He melted small amounts of metal in a wood fire and concluded that the Indians probably were capable of casting; they could have made molds from wood ash (which holds its shape when dried), poured in molten metal, and made beads. A great deal more work is needed, but Leader's problem-solving studies of metal working are an excellent example of how specific questions pertaining to Florida's ancient inhabitants can be addressed using modern investigative techniques.

OTHER ANALYSES

All archaeological sites in Florida will not contain all of the components described above; for example, sites in South Florida rarely contain chert artifacts. On the other hand, archaeological remains sometimes call for special kinds of analyses as diverse as the study of art styles and soils. The archaeological record itself dictates what needs to be examined and the list appears interminable: human osteology, settlement patterns, climate, architecture, and more, including some questions that have not been raised yet. The key is to keep an open mind.

FOUR

 DATING ARTIFACTS AND ARCHAEOLOGICAL SITES

It is amazing how often an archaeologist is able to answer the question "How old is it?" when someone asks about the age of an artifact or a site. If the age of an artifact or a site is not known, it is difficult to know where it fits in the overall heritage of an area. Archaeologists, therefore, are very interested in developing techniques, or using techniques already available, to place sites and their contents in the correct **chronological position**. Many people do not realize how much they depend on historic documents that tell of past events, monuments, artifacts, and important individuals. Most archaeology in North America must be conducted without help from such records because the native peoples did not have written languages. For that reason it is nearly impossible for archaeologists interested in **prehistory** to identify individuals or events from the surviving archaeological record. The purpose of this chapter is to present the different dating methods used by archaeologists.

Three major methods are used to provide an answer to "How old is it?": comparative, relative, and absolute (**chronometric** or **calendric**). The first two, comparative and relative, were used *long* before any chronometric techniques were developed.

COMPARATIVE DATING

At least 100 years ago in America, archaeologists began to classify artifacts, particularly stone spearheads and pottery, on their styles, shapes, and designs. They concluded that those sharing similar shapes, designs, and other characteristics would be of the same general age. The comparative method was refined through the years as more and more artifacts were found and archaeologists became familiar with the kinds of sites from which the artifacts were recovered. There was no way, of course, to say how old the artifacts were, but these early classifications and observations were very important when precise dating techniques became available. Even today, lacking good **context**, experienced archaeologists can give you an accurate description of a specimen found in their region. For instance, if you showed me a Florida spearhead like those illustrated in chapter 1, I could tell you how old it is, what it is made of, how it was made, what kinds of sites it is typically found at, and much more.

RELATIVE DATING

If an archaeological site is excavated correctly, it is usually possible to note that there are different **strata** as layers are skimmed off one by one using arbitrary or natural **stratigraphy**. Natural stratigraphy can be either geologic or cultural (see chapter 2). Assuming that older materials will be deposited first, and thus recovered from lower strata with younger materials accumulating in upper layers, an archaeologist can say (usually) that artifacts found in the bottom of a deposit are older than those found at the top. But, as with the comparative method, there is no way to assign a calendar date to the finds. The best an archaeologist can say is that one item is older or younger than another.

Using combinations of the comparative and relative dating methods, a technique called **seriation** was developed. Seriation is based largely on changes that are observed to occur in artifact types. Seriation works because humans are always changing the way they do things and make things. Sometimes changes take place only after a very long time but in other cases, particularly in technology, changes in style and design may take place rapidly. Since stone and ceramic artifacts are usually found in greater abundance than other objects, seriation has been applied almost exclusively to these materials. Pottery and/or spearheads from individual sites or locations are arranged into a sequence based on their percentages of occurrences as they increase and finally disappear through time as they gain or lose popularity. Although it is not possible to tell early from late without other information such as radiocarbon dates (see below) or a good stratigraphic sequence, seriation provides a useful way to establish control over large masses of material (Jennings 1989).

Extinct plants and, particularly, animals, have been used to assign relative dates to archaeological materials. An excellent example of the use of the fossil record to date the antiquity of cultural remains in the Americas was the discovery in 1927 of stone spearheads in association with extinct bison *(Bison antiquus)* and later with extinct mammoths and mastodons (elephants). These finds proved beyond any doubt that people had been in the Western Hemisphere for thousands of years, although at the time no absolute date could be assigned. We now know that this association of extinct animals with artifacts is at least 11,400 years old.

CHRONOMETRIC DATING

Radiocarbon Dating

In 1949, a revolutionary event took place. Willard F. Libby (Arnold and Libby 1949) developed the radiocarbon method, making it possible for the first time to date organic materials as old as 50,000 years. Archaeology benefited more than any other science from the development of the radiocarbon method, especially the archaeology of the Americas, where radiocarbon determinations span the entire length of human presence in the Western Hemisphere, which probably does not exceed 30,000 years.

Radiocarbon analysis is based on the fact that all living organisms (plants and animals) maintain a constant amount of radioactive carbon (carbon 14) that disintegrates at a known rate after an organism dies. The rate of decay is determined by the half-life of carbon 14, which Libby estimated to be 5,568 years. For consistency, this figure is still used by dating laboratories, even though a more accurate figure is 5,730 years. This simply means that one-half of the radioactive carbon decays every 5,730 years after the death of a plant or animal. So by calculating how much carbon 14 remained in an organic specimen from an archaeological site, Libby was able to determine, within a range, an accurate age for that specimen. If one-fourth of the carbon 14 is still present, an object would be 11,460 years old; if one-eighth is present it would be 17,190 years old; and so on. Obviously, when too much time has passed, the amount of radioactive carbon is very small and its accuracy is less convincing. Thus after 34,380 years only 1/64th remains in a specimen. The half-lives of other radioactive isotopes are too great or not great enough to date the time periods when humans inhabited the New World. For instance, uranium 238 has a half-life of millions of years and tritium has a half-life that is only $12\frac{1}{2}$ years. Potassium-argon has been used to date deposits in volcanic areas in Africa to establish the time that early humans first evolved.

Some organic materials are better to use for radiocarbon dating than others: charcoal, plant remains, wood, bone, and shell, in descending order of confidence. The reason that charred plant remains are the most desirable to date by radiocarbon analysis is because charcoal is chemically inert and because plants absorb radiocarbon directly from the atmosphere whereas animals derive this radioactive source from eating plants. Seasonal plant remains, such as hickory nuts or acorns, may be more accurate than wood from a tree that was alive for 100 years or longer before it died naturally or was cut and used by people in the past. The dating laboratory needs only a few grams of some materials, while a much larger sample is needed for other materials such as bone and for objects that are thought to be very old. When collecting specimens that are to be dated by carbon 14 analysis, care should be taken not to contaminate the samples. The radiocarbon dating laboratory, however, does an excellent job of removing observable potential contaminants such as modern rootlets. If an object has been preserved with any kind of a substance (varnish, linseed oil, glue, etc.) DO NOT try to have it dated.

After an object is dated, the radiocarbon laboratory sends the results as shown in the following example:

$$5000 \pm 100 \text{ years B.P.}$$

It is important that you understand what the date means. First of all, the initials B.P. stand for "before present." The "present" from which dates are measured is A.D. 1950, the year that radiocarbon analysis was born. The date of 5000 ± 100 means that there is a 68 percent probability (one sigma standard deviation) that the date will range from 4900 to 5100 B.P. if the same sample is rerun. In order to increase the probability to 95 percent confidence (two sigmas), the ± date would be increased. So instead of 5000 ± 100, the date of the specimen may be given as 5000 ± 200 B.P. or 4800 – 5200 B.P. With archaeological materials as old as 5,000 years, this range of accuracy is not much of a problem, but obviously if one is dealing with very young materials (only a few hundred years old), this much of a statistical error renders the date practically useless for age interpretation and archaeologists must then rely on other information to date their site or artifacts.

The few grams of carbon-containing material that is needed to obtain a date by radiocarbon analysis may not seem like very much, but often there are not enough surviving organic remains available, or the archaeologist is hesitant about submitting an important specimen for dating because the procedure destroys the material. Fortunately, another technique has been developed in which samples weighing only a few milligrams can be dated. This technique is called accelerator mass spectrometer (AMS) and is very complex. It uses a tandem particle accelerator to measure the individual carbon 14 atoms from a sample to derive a radiocarbon age. By this method, a single seed or tiny bits of charcoal can be dated. A single thread was sacrificed from the controversial Turin Shroud to learn its age by AMS. The cost of such analysis is approximately twice that of normal radiocarbon dating.

One of Libby's basic assumptions about the radiocarbon method was that the concentration of carbon 14 in the atmosphere had been constant through time, but we now know that it has varied because of changes in the geomagnetic field and cosmic radiation. Tree-ring dating (dendrochronology) has furnished a way to calibrate radiocarbon dates (see below) and is also the most accurate of all dating methods (except historic records).

Dendrochronology

Although carbon-14 dating is the most common method used, there are numerous other techniques that have been developed and used in areas where conditions exist that favor their application. In the dry American Southwest, tree-ring dating has provided a cultural chronology that extends back more than 2,000 years and an environmental record more than 8,000 years old. By counting the growth rings of trees that accumulate year by year, tree-ring dating can be used with almost as much accuracy as a calendar.

A master calendar of rings has been built up from hundreds of samples of specimens whose rings are matched backward from living trees known to have been cut in certain years. A specimen can be dated by matching its ring pattern against this sequence. The method works because the sequence consists of broad and narrow rings that are shared by all trees of that species in an area. Although other factors are involved, such as sunlight, broad rings generally occur during years of greater rainfall and narrow rings during times of drought. Thus, tree rings also furnish a climatic record through time. In fact, the astronomer A.E. Douglass, who in his early days dug in mounds on Florida's east coast, originally initiated the study of tree rings in 1914 in his research with sun spots.

Dendrochronology, of course, depends upon having quantities of well-preserved wood with enough tree rings available to fit into an already developed sequence. It also depends upon a variability in pattern distinct enough to be matched against the master record. In the southeastern United States, including Florida, wood seldom survives because of the humid climate, and even if it did survive the ring patterns might be too uniform to establish a sequence. It may be possible to apply tree-ring dating to some of the 250+ ancient canoes made of pine that have been recovered in Florida since many have come from a fairly restricted geographic area. This investigation awaits an energetic researcher! Tree-ring analysis of cypress has been conducted in the Florida Everglades in an attempt to document environmental changes.

By the use of tree-ring dating, archaeologists have been able to determine the exact year that some of the Southwestern pueblos were built. Tree-ring studies are underway in other areas of the world where conditions are favorable.

The real value of dendrochronology to the archaeological profession, however, has derived from the establishment of a 8,000-year tree-ring sequence from the bristlecone pine of California and other species. Since tree-ring counts are very accurate, the 8,000-year sequence made it possible to calibrate the results of dendrochronology to radiocarbon analysis and to determine that cosmic radiation and the geomagnetic field have fluctuated through time. In this way, radiocarbon dates extending to approximately 8,000 years have become more accurate. Some radiocarbon dating laboratories (for example, Beta Analytic, Inc., Miami, Florida) now provide dendro-calibration of all samples in the 8,000-year time range along with a graph accompanying each date to illustate the relationship between radiocarbon and calendar ages (see sample in fig. 4.1). The measurement of a carbon-13/12 ratio is recommended to allow calculation of more accurate calendar age correlations. (Carbon 13 and carbon 12 are stable carbon isotopes.) The laboratory uses an estimated value when a carbon 13/12 ratio is not measured.

Obsidian Hydration

Obsidian is a volcanic glass that occurs in many parts of the world but not in the eastern United States, including Florida. Obsidian is an extremely desirable material that was used by aboriginal peoples for thousands of years to fashion chipped stone implements and even ornaments. The composition of obsidian from a single volcanic flow is very **homogeneous.** Its composition can be determined through techniques such as neutron activation analysis

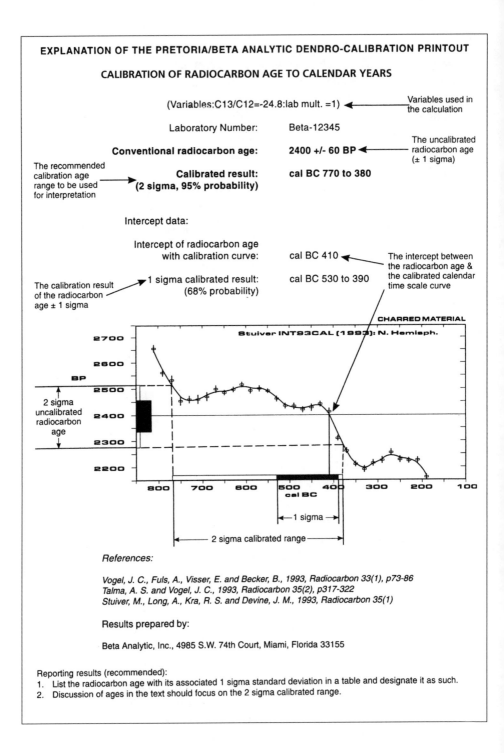

EXPLANATION OF THE PRETORIA/BETA ANALYTIC DENDRO-CALIBRATION PRINTOUT

CALIBRATION OF RADIOCARBON AGE TO CALENDAR YEARS

(Variables:C13/C12=-24.8:lab mult. =1) ◄———— Variables used in the calculation

Laboratory Number: Beta-12345

Conventional radiocarbon age: **2400 +/- 60 BP** ◄———— The uncalibrated radiocarbon age (± 1 sigma)

The recommended calibration age range to be used for interpretation ——► **Calibrated result:** **cal BC 770 to 380**
(2 sigma, 95% probability)

Intercept data:

Intercept of radiocarbon age with calibration curve: cal BC 410 ◄———— The intercept between the radiocarbon age & the calibrated calendar time scale curve

The calibration result of the radiocarbon age ± 1 sigma ——► 1 sigma calibrated result: cal BC 530 to 390
(68% probability)

CHARRED MATERIAL

Stuiver INT93CAL (1993): N. Hemisph.

2 sigma uncalibrated radiocarbon age

BP

2700
2600
2500
2400
2300
2200

800 700 600 500 400 300 200 100
cal BC

◄—1 sigma—►

◄———— 2 sigma calibrated range ————►

References:

Vogel, J. C., Fuls, A., Visser, E. and Becker, B., 1993, Radiocarbon 33(1), p73-86
Talma, A. S. and Vogel, J. C., 1993, Radiocarbon 35(2), p317-322
Stuiver, M., Long, A., Kra, R. S. and Devine, J. M., 1993, Radiocarbon 35(1)

Results prepared by:

Beta Analytic, Inc., 4985 S.W. 74th Court, Miami, Florida 33155

Reporting results (recommended):
1. List the radiocarbon age with its associated 1 sigma standard deviation in a table and designate it as such.
2. Discussion of ages in the text should focus on the 2 sigma calibrated range.

Derivation of a radiometric or accelerator dendro-calibrated (CALENDAR) date requires use of a CONVENTIONAL radiocarbon date (Stuiver and Polach)[1]. The conventional date is a basic radiocarbon date that has been normalized to the modern standard through the use of C13/C12 ratios* (analyzed or estimated). The statistical error (+/-) on an analyzed C13/C12 value is quite small and does not contribute significantly to the combined error on the date. However , use of an estimated C13/C12 ratio for an unknown sample may incur a very large combined error term. This is clearly illustrated in the figure below (Gupta & Polach; modified by J. Head)[2] where the possible range of C13/C12 values for a particular material type may be so large as to preclude any practical application or correction.

In cases where analyzed C13/C12 values are not available, we have provided (for illustration) dendro-calibrations assuming a mean "chart" value, but without an estimated error term.

Where a sample carbon reservoir different from the modern oxalic acid/wood modern standard (e.g. shell) is involved, a further correction must be employed; the necessary variables are displayed on the calibration sheet.

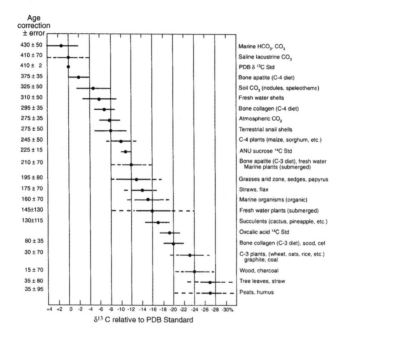

Age correction ± error

Age correction ± error	Material
430 ± 50	Marine HCO$_3$, CO$_3$
410 ± 70	Saline lacustrine CO$_3$
410 ± 2	PDB δ ^{13}C Std
375 ± 35	Bone apatite (C-4 diet)
325 ± 50	Soil CO$_2$ (nodules, speleothems)
310 ± 50	Fresh water shells
295 ± 35	Bone collagen (C-4 diet)
275 ± 35	Atmospheric CO$_2$
275 ± 50	Terrestrial snail shells
245 ± 50	C-4 plants (maize, sorghum, etc.)
225 ± 15	ANU sucrose ^{14}C Std
210 ± 70	Bone apatite (C-3 diet), fresh water Marine plants (submerged)
195 ± 80	Grasses arid zone, sedges, papyrus
175 ± 70	Straws, flax
160 ± 70	Marine organisms (organic)
145±130	Fresh water plants (submerged)
130±115	Succulents (cactus, pineapple, etc.)
	Oxcalic acid ^{14}C Std
80 ± 35	Bone collagen (C-3 diet), sood, cel
30 ± 70	C-3 plants, (wheat, oats, rice, etc.) graphite, coal
15 ± 70	Wood, charcoal
35 ± 80	Tree leaves, straw
35 ± 95	Peats, humus

+4 +2 0 -2 -4 -6 -8 -10 -12 -14 -16 -18 -20 -22 -24 -26 -28 -30%

δ^{13} C relative to PDB Standard

[1] Stuiver, M. and Polach, H.A., 1977. Discussion: Reporting of 14-C data, Radiocarbon, 19, 355-363.

[2] Gupta S.K. and Polach H.A., 1985. Radiocarbon dating practices at ANU Handbook, p. 114. Radiocarbon Laboratory, Research School of Pacific Studies, ANU, Canberra.

*Radiocarbon is incorporated into various materials by different pathways and this introduces differing degrees of isotropic fractionation. The C13/C12 ratio of any material is the millesimal difference of the sample to the carbonate PDB standard and is directly related to the C14/C12 ratio. The degree of sample C-14 enrichment or depletion then is normalized to that of the modern standard.

4.1. Calibration of radiocarbon age to calendar years.

(see chapter 3). When obsidian weathers, it forms a **hydrated** layer on the outer surface that accumulates at a constant, uniform rate and can be measured. Obsidian hydration dating, like dendrochronology, must be worked out on a regional basis because the accumulation of the weathered layer is subject not only to its composition but also to local climatic and soil conditions that differ significantly from region to region.

While obsidian hydration dating is not as universally applicable as radiocarbon dating, it has been accepted as a valid technique in areas where scientists have studied its composition and regional conditions. By calculating the rate of accumulation of the hydrated layer it is possible to assign a time to its use. By comparing the differences in hydrated layers from specimen to specimen, different time periods for the use of an archaeological site or sites can be determined.

Chert Weathering

In Florida we have observed that chert also weathers and forms a fairly uniform layer on the outer surface that is apparent when a specimen is broken (see chapter 3). This layer is not a result of hydration but occurs because certain elements are leached out, particularly iron. We call this a patinated layer, which, like obsidian, can be measured. Because chert or flint materials are not as homogeneous as obsidian, there has been a great deal of controversy about whether or not the patinated layer can be dated. The local conditions of soil and climate, of course, have to be determined as with obsidian hydration. Investigations pertaining to dating of weathered Florida chert have been underway off and on for 20 years, but adequate funding to support a knowledgeable, dedicated researcher and laboratory facilities has not been available. The successful development of a method to date Florida chert would provide a chronology for sites lacking organic materials that are normally used for radiocarbon analysis and could furnish a check on the accuracy of radiocarbon dates from sites where organic materials have been preserved.

Thermoluminescence

This method has been developed to date materials such as ceramics and burnt stone. The successful use of the thermoluminescent (TL) technique to date **inorganic** archaeological specimens depends upon two conditions: (1) an object must have been heated in the past, and (2) it must have luminescent properties.

Crystalline materials contain small amounts of radioactive elements such as uranium, thorium, and potassium that decay at a steady rate and emit alpha, beta, and gamma radiation. This radiation bombards the crystalline structure and displaces electrons, which become trapped in imperfections in the crystalline lattice. When pottery clays are fired or when flints are heated as around a hearth or for purposes of thermal alteration (see chapters 1 and 3), the trapped electrons are discharged in the form of light (luminescence). When this first heating of a geologic material—that is, clay or flint—takes place, the TL "clock" is reset to zero and begins to accumulate trapped electrons again from that time forward. An age can be assigned to an object by knowing the radioactive content of a sample and how susceptible a particular crystalline material is to radiation damage (that is, the rate of accumulation of trapped electrons) and by measuring in the laboratory how much radiation has been stored since the first heating. It is important also to distinguish the amount and kinds of other sources of radiation that may have contributed radiation damage to a sample. The soil from which a specimen is recovered, for example, may be highly radioactive and may add to the radioactivity that comes from impurities within the sample itself, that is, the self dose. For this reason, if an archaeologist plans to have specimens from a site dated by TL, surrounding soil needs to be collected for evaluation at the same time. Otherwise it would be difficult to place much confidence in the accuracy of the resulting TL date.

In Florida, experiments have been conducted to test the feasibility of dating heat-altered cherts by thermoluminescence. The results have been promising but need further refinement. We have been particularly interested in dating chert materials that range from approximately 5,000 to 10,000 years old because many artifacts from this long time period are similar in style, and it is too easy to collapse 5,000 years of time when there is no way to date these specimens more accurately. Often, organic materials do not survive that could be used for radiocarbon analysis. Thermoluminescent dating of Florida Indian ceramics has also been attempted with fairly good success. At Hontoon Island, for example, results of TL analysis of pottery sherds correlated precisely with expected dates and with results received from radiocarbon analysis of associated materials.

You may conclude correctly that very specialized equipment and highly trained experts are needed to conduct TL dating. There are several laboratories in Europe that are doing TL research, but at the present time there is little interest in the method in the Western Hemisphere. It has great promise but little support. A major reason for the lack of support is that radiocarbon dating spans the entire length of human presence in the Americas.

An important application of TL is not for dating at all but for the authentication of art objects that are suspected of having been faked. There are talented but unscrupulous people who wish to make money by selling reproductions of famous ancient ceramic pieces to museums or individuals. Some museums now have TL equipment and personnel that are able to detect fakes by extracting a tiny sample from a ceramic piece and by measuring the amount of light given off when the sample is heated. The art object is probably a fake if little or no luminescence is emitted.

In summary, thermoluminescence (1) can date inorganic materials if they have been heated in the past and if the TL clock has been reset to zero by the heating, (2) provide a check on the reliability of radiocarbon dates, (3) date materials older than the 50,000-year limit of radiocarbon analysis, and (4) authenticate certain works of art. One of the disadvantages of thermoluminescence as a dating method is that it has a greater range of error than radiocarbon dating, but this range may be reduced by future experimentation.

Electron spin resonance is similar to TL in that it depends upon accumulated radiation damage. The method is still in the experimental stage.

Other Chronometric Dating Techniques

Archaeomagnetism is a method that has not been attempted in Florida but might be used at some archaeological sites if the right conditions exist. It depends upon variations in the earth's magnetic field and has been applied to dating clay hearths or kilns when the heated clay has not been moved from its precise spot of firing (see Jennings 1989 for a fuller discussion).

Numerous additional methods have been tried from time to time in an effort to solve the chronology problem of prehistory. Many are still being investigated, such as amino acid racemization, and many have been abandoned as not reliable or practical. All in all, archaeologists today are better able to furnish accurate dates for sites or objects than they were 50 years ago.

FIVE

 DEGRADATION, PRESERVATION, AND CURATION

Three major steps need to be taken to assure the long-term survival of material objects recovered from archaeological sites: (1) determine how much degradation occurred before and after an item became part of the archaeological record, (2) arrange for the application of proper conservation methods to restore and preserve the artifacts and **ecofacts**, and (3) plan for the future **curation** of specimens.

ORGANIC MATERIALS

Degradation

Observe a piece of wood lying on the surface of the ground in your backyard in Florida. You will note that severe changes take place within a year. If you were to watch this same piece of wood for five years, you might discover that it had disappeared. The results of your experiment would depend on the wood species, the size of the object, the location on the tree from which it came, how it was used before it was left on the ground, the climatic conditions over a five-year period, and much more. But one fact is certain: since wood is an

organic material, it is going to degrade in Florida's humid climate. The same statement can be made about all plant remains (seeds, nuts, berries, vines) that people collected and processed as part of their diet or for use as pigments, medicines, and cordage to make woven items such as baskets.

Bone usually does not degrade as rapidly as plant material unless it becomes incorporated into an acid soil, such as a peat deposit. Bone contains **calcium carbonate,** which decomposes in the presence of acid.

Shell, like bone, is composed of calcium carbonate and may dissolve under certain circumstances, but generally it is very durable. Archaeologists have observed postdepositional modification of marine shell caused by leaching of calcium carbonate due to the effect of humic acids and groundwater in the soil. Specimens have a chalky texture and wear patterns are eroded. Also, soil concretions may become cemented on the surface of shell tools, and peeling of some of the growth layers on the ventral surface may occur. These noncultural alterations can hinder interpretation of manufacture and use. On the other hand, Cushing (1897) observed deep furrows on shell tools where wooden handles were secured with rawhide ("now mere jelly"). He interpreted these as marks resulting from wear, but the marks may have been visible because the rawhide had disintegrated underwater and corroded the shell where it had been in contact with the lashings. The species of marine shellfish commonly used for producing tools and ornaments, such as *Busycon* (busycon) and *Mercenaria* (quahog), are very resistant to degradation. In Florida, freshwater shellfish species were seldom made into artifacts. Because shell does not degrade or break easily, it usually needs very little care or curation.

When one considers how important plants and animals are to the diet and **technologies** of people everywhere (even today), it is easy to conclude how much of the archaeological record is lost (about 95 percent) if these materials do not survive. Obviously, one cannot study something that has disappeared. An archaeological treasure house exists when favorable conditions occur in the natural environment that prevent the degradation of plant and animal remains. These situations can be found in locations that remain continuously frozen, wet, or dry. In Florida, there are many wet sites, but Florida, of course, has no locations that are constantly dry or frozen.

Preservation

Botanical materials that survive at archaeological wet sites in Florida appear to be very well preserved, but most of their structure has been lost through the years and replaced by water. When these items are removed from the wet soil that has protected them, they will disintegrate in a very short time (within 12 hours) if they are not cared for properly.

The best nontoxic product known at present to preserve waterlogged wood is polyethylene glycol (PEG). It is a synthetic polymer similar to antifreeze that you might use in the radiator of your car if you lived in a cold climate. A product such as PEG is needed to fill the void left in the cells and cell walls of wooden objects after they are removed from their saturated environment. As mentioned above, wood often appears very sturdy while it is still waterlogged, but if it is allowed to dry out before it is treated, it shrinks dramatically, splinters, warps, and loses about 90 percent of its waterlogged weight. At this stage, the process cannot be reversed because the cells and cell walls have collapsed (see fig. 3.2b). A formula that has been used successfully to preserve waterlogged wood with PEG is:

1   Keep the wood wet until treatment begins.
2   Mix 10 percent solution of PEG with water. There are various molecular weights available. I have had good luck using PEG 540 Blend, a product from Union Carbide Corporation (Carbowax).
3   Increase the concentration of PEG by 10 percent each month until the solution reaches about 80 percent PEG. The length of time at each concentration really depends on the size and condition of the objects being preserved. It is important to be patient so that the PEG will penetrate the wood and add support to its structure. Be sure to stir the mixture gently every day or so to keep the PEG from settling to the bottom.

If you discover that this formula does not work for the wood you are attempting to preserve, then you need to experiment further.

Superior results have been obtained by scientists who use freeze-drying in conjunction with PEG to preserve wooden artifacts. The size of the objects is restricted by the size of the freeze-drying apparatus. Because of natural freeze-drying conditions in the high Andes of South America, the Andean Indians have been freeze-drying potatoes for hundreds, maybe thousands, of years.

PEG is used also to preserve cordage, nets, and baskets, but these items require a different molecular weight than that described above. Another product, however, was used to preserve the 7,000–8,000-year-old textiles recovered from 37 of the burials at the Windover Site near Titusville. These textiles represent some of the oldest in the Western Hemisphere. A combination of freeze-drying and parylene conformal coating appears to be the most effective way to conserve these very fragile fabric remains, which were probably manufactured from fibers of the Sabal palm.

Sugar is an inexpensive substance that can be used as a preservative for waterlogged wood. It has been effective in treating canoes and other large objects when the price of PEG is prohibitive. Unfortunately, sugar attracts insects and other organisms, which then necessitates the use of a toxic compound (copper sulfate, for example) to prevent their invasion of the wood during and after it is treated. The presence of this toxic chemical in the preservation vat can cause an environmental problem when the vat is emptied after preservation is completed. Another difficulty with sugar is that it tends to carmelize with low temperatures over a long period of time, especially if it is reused.

Many other problems may arise in preserving wood from water-saturated sites. For instance, objects that have survived at offshore shipwrecks may need special care because of salt water or because items are made up of more than one material such as wood and metal combinations.

Plant materials other than wood that have survived at archaeological wet sites also will disintegrate if not kept in water or treated with a botanical preservative (formaline alcohol acetic acid) immediately after they are removed from their waterlogged environment.

Bone is much more durable than wood. For example, there are bone objects in storage and on exhibit at the Florida Museum of Natural History in Gainesville that were collected 50 to 100 years ago. They have not been treated and are still in good condition. To be on the safe side, however, it is recommended that bone be dipped in a solution of a polyvinyl acetate emulsion (Elmer's Glue or a similar product—3 parts water to 1 part glue) and then allowed to dry on a nonsticking surface. This procedure is particularly important for small bones such as those from fish recovered at archaeological wet sites because they tend to curl up if not treated. Fossil bone may require different preservation methods.

Curation

Archaeological wood and other organic materials need to be monitored frequently to assure their survival so that future generations can study and enjoy them. In the event that the preservation of wood and textiles was not totally successful or if objects are attacked by organisms, a curator should be able to notice signs of deterioration in time to correct the problem. Botanical remains that have been kept waterlogged or submerged in a chemical solution need to be checked from time to time to be certain the liquid has not evaporated and desiccated (dried) the specimens.

Very often the way artifacts are preserved and curated depends upon their value to the institution or individual responsible for their care. A study collection kept in storage may not receive the same attention as exhibit-quality objects. At one large museum, however, several wooden masks and figurines that had fallen from the wall to the floor of the display case lay there disintegrating for an unknown amount of time before the situation was called to the attention of the museum director. The point is that these fragile objects need to have provisions made for their survival for centuries to come. Their loss would be similar to the destruction of Greek statues. Florida does not have stone, such as marble, suitable for making statues, so the early Indian people of Florida used wood to produce large art objects.

STONE

Degradation

Stone is very durable and because of this it is often the only material that has survived the ravages of time to provide evidence that people were present in an area. In Florida, for example, nearly all of the information that exists about the Paleoindian period (about 11,000–9,000 B.P.) comes from stone remains.

The kind of stone that was used to make spearheads (usually flint, chert) fractures like glass, so many stone points are broken when found; that is, they were broken thousands of years ago by hunters or warriors and thrown away. Flint tools can also undergo further damage caused by the environment in which they have been discarded. For instance, if they are lost in a river they may be shattered when water moves them along and they bump into hard objects in the stream bed. And even though stone is very durable, it can **weather** under certain circumstances. Sometimes the weathering is so extreme that the flake scars are removed (see chapter 3). One kind of weathering is called patina formation (see chapter 3) and might actually be used to date stone artifacts under very controlled conditions (see chapter 4 for an explanation).

Florida Indians did not make tools, weapons, or ornaments from other kinds of rock, such as granite or greenstone, because suitable rock for these purposes is not native to Florida. Thus, when artifacts such as these are found in Florida, one can conclude that they were imported.

Preservation

All in all, stone artifacts can remain in a museum drawer or on exhibit for hundreds of years without undergoing any noticeable change. Under normal circumstances, no conservation techniques need to be applied. However, in areas other than Florida where there are buildings and statues made of stones (marble and limestone, for example) that are not as durable as flint, such as in Egypt and Greece, damage has resulted from earthquakes, volcanoes, weathering, and vandalism. Some scientists specialize in developing and applying methods to prevent further destruction of these monuments and to restore those that have been harmed.

Curation

Stone implements, particularly those made of flint materials, should be stored carefully so they do not fracture. Like gemstones and precious metals, spearheads are fascinating, and museums must watch out for theft. Stone implements are valuable because they are durable and because their styles provide excellent information about time periods and limited insights about the activities of early people. Museums often do not have complete collections of stone implements for study or exhibit because pothunters like spearheads, which they hoard while leaving other significant materials in their **spoil piles**. Sometimes, unfortunately, spearheads are traded back and forth among collectors so that eventually no one remembers where they came from in the first place.

CERAMICS

Degradation

Ceramic artifacts are made of clays that have been fired to temperatures high enough to cause permanent changes in the clay. Before the clay is fired, it can be shaped into endless kinds of large or small utilitarian and artistic objects. This important technology was introduced into Florida more than 4,000 years ago. Florida ceramics have been studied intently by archaeologists for about 100 years. (For information about ceramic styles and designs, see chapter 1.) Unfortunately, the Florida Indians never developed **pyrotechniques** or ceramic technology to a high level of excellence as did, for instance, the people of China. As a result, their ceramic pieces broke easily and whole pots are seldom recovered at archaeological sites in Florida except in burial mounds.

Because Florida clays were poorly fired and contain a fairly large amount of sand or other inclusions called temper, the ceramics made from these clays are **friable** and tended to weather before and after they became part of the archaeological record.

Preservation

Very often, enough broken pieces (sherds) of a single pottery bowl are recovered during excavations so that it can be glued back together. In this way, sizes, shapes, and functions can be determined from restored objects, adding important information about past human activities. Ceramic artifacts are found in abundance at archaeological sites younger than 4000 B.P. They are sometimes the only artifacts found during excavations. Their value lies in the fact that they can provide clues about the typical "dishes" used at a site during a particular time period or about trade relations if a few nonlocal styles are present also (see chapter 1 for examples).

Curation

Ceramic artifacts usually remain stable after they are placed in storage at museums. The most important aspects of curation are to keep them together by the location where they were found so they can be studied and restored and to prevent them from crumbling because of their friable nature. Spectacular specimens are usually placed on exhibit.

METALS

Degradation, Preservation, and Curation

Metal ores such as copper, silver, gold, and iron are not native to the state of Florida. Before the conquest of the Americas in A.D. 1492, the only metal that was used in Florida was copper, which was traded in from other areas in completed form (see examples in chapter 1). Artifacts made of copper are not very abundant in Florida, and they are usually found in an advanced state of degradation that necessitates careful application of several kinds of preservation efforts, including electrolysis. The most fragile pieces are encapsulated in a clear Plexiglass container that is made inert by purging it of oxygen so that air is exchanged with argon under pressure. Thus, treatment is not attempted but the objects are no longer subjected to degrading processes.

Gold, silver, and iron objects are found at sites that date after A.D. 1500 and probably came from shipwrecks off of Florida's coasts. Gold "shines forever," as the saying goes, and usually is found in fairly good condition, as is silver, although silver will tarnish. Because of oxidation, iron is usually soft, rusty, and corroded when recovered. It can be treated by electrolysis if some solid metal remains. The piece to be preserved is placed in a container lined with fiberglass and then filled with water and a 2 percent solution of caustic acid. It is attached to a negative charge. The negative chloride ions are mobile and migrate out toward the positive pole, which results in a loosening of the encrustations from the iron. Iron objects such as nails usually take about 30 days to treat, whereas it takes two years to preserve cannons or other large items. After preservation, the objects are coated with a wax or lacquer to prevent future corrosion. Electrolysis will not completely return iron artifacts to their original shape. Glass beads and European ceramics, both introduced after A.D. 1500, need very little curation.

The most important aspects of curation are to prevent theft of the precious metals (gold and silver) while they are in storage or on exhibit and to monitor them for signs of degradation such as tarnish on silver objects and too much atmospheric moisture that might affect iron pieces.

SUMMARY

The native peoples of Florida used materials from the natural environment for food and to produce objects that were needed or desired for their survival. Most of the materials—stone, shell, and fired clay—resist degradation to a greater or lesser extent and endure storage and exhibit conditions with a minimum of care. Organic remains, however, particularly plants, are preserved in Florida only in locations that have remained permanently waterlogged. They require immediate and continuous conservation and curation to prevent their disintegration, but the effort is worthwhile if one considers that nearly 95 percent of all items used by societies come from organic materials. The knowledge gained from studying plants and animals recovered from archaeological wet sites fleshes out the past in ways not otherwise possible unless people were still alive who could tell us about it.

$IX

RULES AND REGULATIONS

The American worldview of rugged individualism and the Fifth Amendment to the Constitution, which forbids seizure of private property, are partially responsible for the destruction of sites and the possession of significant antiquities by private citizens. Equally at fault is the folk belief that lost and abandoned property, especially objects of antiquity, treasure trove, coins, and precious metals, belong to the finder regardless of the ownership of the property upon which they are located.

In this chapter I discuss the procedures that must be followed and the restrictions that must be observed if the archaeological resources of the United States are going to be disturbed and explain how these regulations apply specifically to the state of Florida. First I present a brief history of the evolution of legislation designed to protect the nation's heritage "in a spirit of trusteeship for the future" (Jennings 1989:329).

NATIONAL LEGISLATION

By the mid-nineteenth century, some individuals and organizations (e.g., the Smithsonian Institution and the Bureau of American Ethnology) were conscious of the fact that archaeological and natural resources were worthy of preservation and conservation, but it was not until 1906 that Congress passed the Antiquities Act and in 1916 established the National Park Service. As a result, some archaeological sites on public lands were safeguarded. Mesa Verde, an Anasazi "cliff palace" in Colorado, became the first site protected by the government. Mesa Verde was selected because it was magnificent and because it had been vandalized and looted by Richard Wetherill since he first saw it in December 1888.

The Work Projects Administration (WPA) was created in the early 1930s to relieve national unemployment brought about by the Great Depression. The Smithsonian Institution suggested that archaeological projects requiring a large labor force were needed to collect massive amounts of data that would be destroyed during construction of dams, roads, and other public works. In Florida, for example, the Belle Glade site located on the southeastern edge of Lake Okeechobee, although not endangered at that time, was excavated by a large crew supervised by M.W. Stirling with funds provided by the Federal Emergency Relief program. Knowledge of the nation's archaeological remains increased tremendously during this period, although the methods used to excavate were not always praiseworthy.

The Historic Building Survey Act of 1935, the National Trust for Historic Preservation of 1949, and the National Historic Preservation Act (NHPA) of 1966 signaled an "awakening of nationalistic pride in the American past, and a desire to preserve inspirational places and buildings that mark landmark events in national history" (Jennings 1989:329). The Historic Sites Act of 1935 gave the Secretary of the Interior broad historic preservation powers, but it was limited by its focus on nationally significant properties. The NHPA expanded federal agency responsibilities to include the identification, protection, and preservation of archaeological and historic properties of national, regional, state, and local significance. The NHPA, the National Environmental Policy Act (NEPA) of 1969, and the Archaeological Resources Protection Act (ARPA) of 1979 ushered in present-day federal rules and regulations regarding the preservation of the nation's historic and prehistoric resources. Brief descriptions of these acts follow.

National Historic Preservation Act

The National Historic Preservation Act (NHPA) required the federal government to implement a nationwide system for identifying, protecting, and rehabilitating "historic places." The National Register of Historic Places was established, which protects prehistoric sites as well as historic properties. The

NHPA required that each state develop its own historic preservation pro-gram headed by a state historic preservation officer (SHPO). The NHPA also requires the head of each federal agency to take into account the effect of the agency's actions on sites and properties listed or eligible for listing in the Na-tional Register of Historic Places. The process involves consultation with the SHPO and with the Federal Advisory Council on Historic Preservation. Imple-mentation of Executive Order 11593 in 1971 made it mandatory that surveys be conducted and that comprehensive information be prepared and maintained. Federal agencies were ordered to take the lead in historic preservation and to locate properites that might qualify for the National Register. Amendments to the NHPA in 1980 made Executive Order 11593 law, provided for pass-through funds to certified local authorities, and recognized that Indian tribes should have preservation programs and relationships with the National Park Service and the State Historic Preservation offices.

National Environmental Policy Act

The National Environmental Policy Act (NEPA) laid down a comprehensive policy for government land use planning and resource management. It re-quires federal agencies to weigh environmental, historical, and cultural values whenever federally owned land is modified or private land is modified with federal funds. An inventory of archaeological resources would presumably affect future land use planning.

Archaeological Resources Protection Act

The Archaeological Resources Protection Act (ARPA) amended the Antiqui-ties Act of 1906 and was passed in response to increasing looting of cultural resources to feed a growing antiquities market. The ARPA made it a felony to remove archaeological materials from federal lands without a permit. In re-cent years, amendments to the ARPA have tightened definitions of what con-stitutes archaeological resources and have legislated more severe penalties. The ARPA gives no protection to archaeological resources on privately owned land.

Native American Graves Protection and Repatriation Act

On 16 November 1990, President George Bush signed into law the Native American Graves Protection and Repatriation Act (Pub. L. 101–601; 25 U.S.C. 3001–3013; 104 Stat. 3048–3058). This act gives lineal descendants and mem-bers of Indian tribes the right to certain Native American human remains and to cultural items with which the human remains are affiliated. It controls or prohibits the inadvertent discovery or intentional excavation of Native American human remains or cultural items on federal or tribal lands. It requires that each federal agency or museum receiving federal funds that possesses human remains or funerary objects of Native American cultural patrimony provide an inventory or summary of the collections to the lineal descendants who may wish to request repatriation of such objects. The Indian tribe should take appropriate steps to make certain that any human remains or cultural items be protected or disposed of (including reburial) in accordance with their ownership. Repatriation may be delayed if there are circumstances in which human remains and cultural items are indispensable to the completion of a specific scientific study commenced prior to receipt of a request for repatriation. There could be severe penalties for violating the provisions of the Native American Graves Protection and Repatriation Act.

Other Legislation

In 1989, important laws established a National Museum of the American Indian and charged the Smithsonian Institution with both setting up this museum and developing policies for the repatriation of skeletal remains held by the institution.

Cultural resources are only part of the complicated but still inadequate legislation governing the effects of human activities on the total landscape. Numerous federal, state, and local agencies are involved at all levels and each has its own regulations. Appropriate agencies should be contacted when answers to specific questions are needed. When these questions pertain to the state of Florida, personnel in the Division of Historical Resources, Tallahassee, are helpful in answering the questions or guiding people to the right organization.

CULTURAL RESOURCE MANAGEMENT

"Cultural resource management is the application of management skills to preserve important parts of our cultural heritage, both historic and prehistoric, for the benefit of the public" (Fagan 1991:494). Although it is sometimes called contract, salvage, rescue, or emergency archaeology, the main function of cultural resource management (CRM) is protection and management. The emergence of the concept of CRM in the 1970s resulted from concern about the loss of these resources and the implementation of legislation, particularly the NHPA and NEPA, to stem that loss.

The NEPA obligates federal agencies to consider the environmental effects of projects under their jurisdiction as part of the federal planning process. The first step in the process results in an environmental assessment (EA). If effects are identified, then a more detailed report—an environmental impact statement (EIS)—is prepared. The historic preservation procedures adopted for EIS documents are those of the NHPA and its implementing regulation 36 CFR 800. Large public works projects, such as new highways and waterworks, require NEPA compliance, as do private projects such as phosphate mining. The NHPA, rather than the NEPA, provides the primary federal historic preservation compliance process. Specifically, Section 106 of the NHPA requires the head of each federal agency to take into account the effect of its actions on National Register and National Register–eligible properties. This process begins with a determination of effect review and involves providing the SHPO an opportunity to comment on the effect, or potential effect, of the proposed undertaking on significant archaeological or historic sites and properties. If an effect or potential effect is identified, the agency must enter into consultation with the SHPO and the Federal Advisory Council on Historic Preservation on measures considered to avoid, minimize, or mitigate any adverse effects.

But who supplies the expertise to carry out the compliance process? Who is qualified to make recommendations about the future of America's cultural heritage? Several professional archaeologists have discussed the chaos that arose from the virtual explosion of requests for professional archaeological services by construction agencies that needed to comply with federal and state historic preservation laws and regulations so they could proceed with their projects. Until the 1970s most archaeologists were academicians who taught courses and conducted research field projects when money and time were available. Many of them were not free to conduct CRM studies or declined to do so because they felt that the "mere search for sites was not the path to knowledge" (Jennings 1989:330). A conflict of interest was created between research-oriented and government-inspired archaeologists. Private companies claiming archaeological skills appeared overnight and began bidding on and receiving contract awards when universities could not accommodate the market. The lowest bidder got the contract regardless of the lack of archaeological training and the poor quality of the reports. No one seemed to care about the national heritage as long as clients and government regulations were satisfied. Guidelines needed to be established to set standards for field and laboratory work and report writing.

The Society of Professional Archaeologists (SOPA) was created in 1976 to set forth a code of ethics for archaeologists and to impose a minimum level of training required to conduct archaeological work. SOPA certifies individuals who can show proof of basic training and also recognizes experience in a number of different specialties. Minimum requirements include at least an M.A. or M.S. in anthropology, plus 12 weeks of supervised fieldwork, 4 weeks of supervised laboratory work, and evidence of the ability to write reports. Specialities or emphases in which certification can be obtained after the minimum requirements are met are field research, collections research, theoretical or archival, archaeological administration, CRM, museology, teaching, marine survey, historical archaeology, underwater archaeology, and archaeometric (physical and natural science) research.

While SOPA guidelines may not always reflect the reality of carrying out archaeology under CRM conditions, the establishment of basic standards and the requirement by many agencies that contractors be certified by SOPA (or meet SOPA standards) has increased the quality of archaeological work in North America. Some CRM projects in recent years, including a number in Florida, have even been able to incorporate problem-oriented research goals into compliance contracts. Nevertheless, second-rate surveys and reports are still accepted sometimes.

"Cultural resource management is now the dominant force in American archaeology, the source of most funds, and the vehicle through which most archaeological research will be effected for many years" (Jennings 1989:333). Thus, it is imperative that the quality of work continues to improve. My opinion is that the preservation of America's natural and cultural heritage has not yet become part of the value system of our society. Protective legislation cannot be the only driving force. We need to develop a national pride and internalize it.

STATE OF FLORIDA HISTORIC PRESERVATION

In 1990, after many recommendations and numerous revisions, the Division of Historical Resources, Florida Department of State, produced *The Historic Preservation Compliance Review Program* (Tesar 1990). It is a 56-page guide (plus appendices) to the historic preservation provisions of state and federal environmental review laws. The main headings in the table of contents are (1) Introduction; (2) Historic Preservation Overview; (3) Historic Preservation

Compliance Review Program; (4) Standards for Conducting, Reporting, and Reviewing Archaeological and Historic Site Assessment Survey Activities; (5) Conclusions; and (6) Appendices. The comments that follow have been summarized from the Tesar document.

The function of the manual is to describe "the manner and procedures for dealing with both prehistoric and historic archaeological sites, historic structures, historic landscapes, and associated features under federal and state environmental impact review laws and regulations." It borrows from comparable federal documents, as part of its purpose is to present a uniform federal-state process. Over 20 Florida statutes have provisions pertaining to the issue of historic preservation. The Florida Historical Resources Act (Chapter 267, *Florida Statutes*) is Florida's primary historic preservation legislation. In many ways it parallels the provisions of the federal National Historic Preservation Act (NHPA) of 1966. Subsections of the Florida Historical Resources Act (1) set forth state policy regarding historic properties and the issue of historic preservation, (2) present historic preservation requirements of state agencies in the executive branch, (3) establish the Division of Historical Resources as Florida's primary historic preservation agency, (4) create the position of State Archaeologist, and (5) create the position of the State Historic Preservation Officer (SHPO).

The four functional units of the Division of Historical Resources are the Bureau of Historic Preservation, the Bureau of Archaeological Research, the Florida Folklife Programs, and the Museum of Florida History. Only the first two are involved in compliance review activities. The Bureau of Archaeological Research (1) administers the Florida Site File, (2) administers the state's shipwreck salvage program, (3) permits conduct of archaeological research on state-owned and state-controlled lands and sovereignty submerged lands (fig. 6.1), (4) assists in the management of archaeological sites on state-owned lands, and (5) curates the agency's artifact collections and archaeological field notes. The bureau chief is the state archaeologist.

The Bureau of Historic Preservation serves as the staff of the SHPO, who provides the first consultation step in reviewing federally involved projects in accordance with the provisions of Section 106 of the NHPA. The bureau is divided into four units: (1) Survey and Registration Section, (2) Architectural Preservation Services, (3) Grants and Education Section, and (4) Historic Preservation Compliance Review Section.

Florida's historic preservation policy includes the elements of identification, evaluation, registration, protection, enhancement, and education. These

Florida Bureau of Archaeological Research
Archaeological Research Permit (Chapter 1A-32) Application Form

Applicant: Project Name:

Address: Application Date:

City: State: Zip:

Principal Investigator: (attach brief resumé)

Project Contact Person: Telephone:

Address:

Site or Project Location: (attach project location map)

Florida Site File number(s):

Property Manager Name:

Address:

City: Phone:

Threats to Resourc

Proposed Work: (attach research design)

Crew Size: Estimated Project Cost:

Source of Funding:

Proposed Beginning Date: Proposed Ending Date: Proposed Report Date:

Publication Outlet(s):

Curatorial Facility:

HRE04404-92
(Note: If underwater or wetlands excavations are involved, provide evidence that dredge and fill permits
(DER and COE) and consent to use state lands (DNR) have been obtained, or determined not necessary.)

6.1. Permit to conduct archaeological research on state-owned and state-controlled lands and sovereignty submerged lands.

various components are described in Tesar (1990). Registration is discussed below under the Florida Site File (FSF).

Not all historic structures or archaeological sites merit full preservation consideration. Such consideration is focused on those sites and properties deemed to be "significant." The significance of archaeological remains and other historic resources is determined by the criteria established for eligibility for listing in the National Register of Historic Places. The compliance review program is a uniform procedure for reviewing projects under the historic preservation requirements of federal and state laws, rules, and regulations. These procedures are discussed fully in Tesar (1990). Florida's historic preservation program attempts to blend preservation with needs for new land uses and construction. It recognizes that total preservation is unrealistic and not always in the public interest.

The Historic Preservation Compliance Review Program is designed to be amended periodically in response to changes in applicable laws and regulations. The newly implemented Native American Graves Protection and Repatriation Act (NAGPRA) is an example of legislation that has been signed into law since the Florida document was prepared. Previous to its passage all unmarked human remains (those not in established cemeteries with tombstones and other markers and monuments) were treated according to the provisions of Chapter 872, *Florida Statutes.* With the passage of the NAGPRA, Indian remains on federal lands and in federally assisted museums must be treated separately.

In addition to the Division of Historical Resources through its several units in Tallahassee, other groups throughout the state are involved in historic preservation efforts. Among these are: the Florida Historical Society, the Florida Anthropological Society, the Florida Archaeological Council (with membership requirements similar to SOPA), the Archaeological Conservancy, the Nature Conservancy, the Trust for Public Lands, the Florida Trust for Historic Preservation, and the Florida Humanities Council. There are many other organizations in the state that are directly or indirectly concerned with natural and cultural preservation, such as the State Park Service. The Conservation and Recreation Lands (CARL) Program is a state land acquisition program. It has been responsible for the acquisition and public protection of hundreds of archaeological sites. The Division of Historical Resources is a member of both the land acquisition and land management advisory committees that recommend actions to the governor and cabinet.

The Florida Bureau of Archaeological Research has worked with the Florida Departments of Law Enforcement, Environmental Protection, and Agriculture as well as the Florida Game and Fish Commission, the National Park Service, the Federal Law Enforcement Training Center, and the Florida Archaeological Council in the design of two training programs. This effort was in response to a legislative mandate to improve the state's archaeological preservation laws and to institute appropriate training for law enforcement personnel within the state. All law enforcement officers undergoing basic training in Florida receive instruction on archaeological resource protection. Recruits are trained in the implementation of chapters 267 and 872 of the *Florida Statutes* concerning archaeological resources on state lands and unmarked human burials. In addition, a special eight-hour archaeological resource protection program has been designed for training officers who are already certified in law enforcement and who can specialize in archaeological cases.

Individuals or organizations interested in or needing information pertaining to rules and regulations governing historic preservation in Florida are urged to write for a copy of *The Historic Preservation Compliance Review Program* to:

Florida Department of State
Division of Historical Resources
Bureau of Historic Preservation
R.A. Gray Building, 500 South Bronough Street
Tallahassee, Florida 32399-0250

The compliance manual also furnishes guidelines for selecting a qualified consultant.

Abandoned Shipwreck Act

It seems appropriate to describe this federal legislation in some detail because it resulted primarily from efforts of the state of Florida to curb the looting of historic shipwrecks that too often masqueraded as underwater archaeology (Fagan 1991:501). In addition, with advances in diving technology and increased leisure time, more people are interested in exploring the underwater world. The information in the following paragraphs is taken from a manuscript prepared by Dr. Roger C. Smith, Bureau of Archaeological Research, Tallahassee.

The Florida Historical Resources Act states that all treasure trove, artifacts, and such objects having historical or archaeological value that have been abandoned on state-owned submerged lands belong to the state. The title to such property is vested in the Division of Historical Resources of the Department of State for purposes of management and protection.

Florida has numerous significant shipwreck sites dating from the early sixteenth century onwards. The approximately 250 shipwreck sites that have been identified and are recorded by the state are believed to represent only about 10 percent of the total number of shipwrecks in Florida's waters. Of those, the small percentage of shipwrecks from between the 1500s and the mid-1800s are considered to have historical significance. An even smaller percentage of these, mainly from Spanish fleet disasters, have been found to contain treasure trove in the form of gold and silver bullion and specie. Commercial salvage, both with and without the permission of the state, has taken place on several Spanish "treasure" galleon sites. This has led to the false public perceptions that most shipwrecks in Florida contain objects of high monetary value and that commercial returns justify their salvage.

In the absence of law to the contrary, Florida, like most states, historically assumed jurisdiction of the management of shipwrecks submerged in the state's waters. Since the 1930s, the state has permitted shipwrecks to be salvaged or explored under contracts with the state. Since 1967, this program has been administered by the Department of State, Division of Historical Resources. Two rules in state law have direct bearing on historic shipwrecks and other archaeological sites.

Chapter 1A-31, Florida Administrative Code, establishes procedures for the exploration and salvage of historic shipwreck sites under contractual agreements with private parties under certain guidelines. The rule provides that no person may conduct operations to explore, excavate, or salvage archaeological materials from shipwrecks without an exploration or salvage agreement issued by the Division of Historical Resources. Participants must first enter an exploration agreement to determine the presence and nature of shipwreck remains within the specified boundaries. If these activities result in a shipwreck discovery, the holder of the exploration contract may seek a salvage contract. The Division of Historical Resources may not enter into such an agreement unless it determines that the applicant seeking the agreement is professionally qualified through demonstration of archaeological ability to conduct such salvage activities and that the find is not of such significance that it should be excavated only by scientifically established research standards.

The rule also states that all archaeological property salvaged is the property of the state. The Division of Historical Resources may pay for the salvage in accordance with the terms of the contract. Generally, the terms have permitted salvors to retain 75 to 80 percent of the artifacts salvaged by value. The Division of Historical Resources is also required to supervise the salvage through proper documentation of all salvaged artifacts. To protect the interests of the state, the Division of Historical Resources limits the number of contracts for salvage to a number that it can properly supervise.

Controversy regarding Florida's management of historic shipwrecks resulted in court decisions that had national implications. Beginning in 1979, a series of federal admiralty actions to claim historic shipwrecks were filed in federal courts in Florida. Federal admiralty law, a product of several hundred years of maritime cases, traditionally provides incentives for vessels to come to the aid of distressed vessels by awarding part of the cargo saved to the rescuing vessel. The law was designed to save lives and merchandise in marine peril and to return salvaged goods to commerce.

Prior to 1979, admiralty law had not generally been applied to historic shipwrecks. In that year, a treasure salvage company filed an admiralty action in federal court in which it sought ownership of a Spanish galleon that had wrecked in 1715 in Florida's sovereign waters. The state filed a counterclaim, and lengthy litigation ensued in which the original admiralty action was extended to include other shipwreck sites in state-owned waters. The foundation of the admiralty claim rested on the fact that federal historic preservation law was silent with respect to historic shipwrecks. When there is a conflict between federal and state law and each law is held to be valid, federal law takes precedence, just as state law does over local ordinances. The U.S. Supreme Court determined that Florida's Chapter 267, *Florida Statutes,* is valid, but in the absence of federal historic preservation law reserving jurisdiction to such resources, admiralty law applied to all classes of shipwrecks and their cargo, regardless of age and other factors. In 1983, the litigation on the 1715 fleet wreck sites was concluded by an out-of-court settlement in which the state agreed to recognize admiralty claims on certain wreck sites. The salvage company agreed to conduct salvage of these sites under certain archaeological guidelines drafted by both parties.

As a result of this and an earlier case, the state's ability to manage its shipwrecks was undermined by salvors continuing to file admiralty actions in federal courts. This occurred not only in Florida; the Florida case affected every state's claim of title to historic shipwrecks. After several attempts to enact laws clarifying state jurisdiction over these resources, Congress finally passed the Abandoned Shipwreck Act of 1987. The federal act awarded title to historic shipwrecks to the United States. Title is then immediately transferred to the individual state in whose waters the shipwreck is submerged. The act clearly exempted the management of historic shipwrecks from federal admiralty law and granted ownership and regulation to the states. In accordance with the act, the National Park Service of the U.S. Department of the Interior issued guidelines in 1990 to assist the states in developing programs to manage historic shipwrecks. The act did not affect existing admiralty claims of shipwreck salvage as long as the claimants with court certified arrests continued to "diligently" work those sites.

It should be noted that Florida has one of the longest-standing programs of underwater archaeology and historic shipwrecks in the country. In fact, several of the Abandoned Shipwreck Act guidelines are based on management policies that have been explored in Florida. These include the establishment of a shipwreck advisory board, the designation of shipwreck reserve areas in which no salvage is allowed, the creation of underwater shipwreck parks, cooperation with recreational divers and fishermen, encouragement of research projects, private sector recovery of shipwrecks consistent with historic preservation standards, and a program of inventory and assessment of underwater resources.

Florida Site File

Registration of sites occurs on two levels. The first is a general record entered into the Florida Site File (FSF), while the second is a listing in the National Register of Historic Places (NRHP). The FSF is a data base of all recorded sites, while the NRHP includes only properties formally determined eligible and listed in the file for their national, state, or local significance individually or as a group. The compliance review staff of the Bureau of Historic Preservation depends heavily on the use of the FSF, which is maintained by the Bureau of Archaeological Research. FSF forms must be completed for all prehistoric and historic sites properties whether or not they are considered significant. Surveys are incomplete until all prehistoric and historic sites and properties are identified and reported (Tesar 1990).

Smith provides detailed information about the Florida Site File (Smith 1989; Smith and Walton 1989). Smith's writings provide instructions about how to complete Survey Log Sheets, Archaeological Site Forms, Historical Structure Forms, and other pertinent forms (such as those concerning cemeteries and bridges). These forms and the introduction to the Florida Site File

Guidelines for Users, dated 22 November 1993, appear at the end of this chapter (figs. 6.2 to 6.6).

Archaeological Site Forms should be used to record all prehistoric and historic archaeological sites. The Historical Structure Form should be used to record all buildings or engineering structures with major structural elements remaining. Sites are designated in the following manner: (1) a state identification number, which is "8" for Florida because Florida was the eighth state alphabetically before Alaska was admitted to the Union; (2) a county identification of two letters, such as AL for Alachua; (3) a site number that is assigned by the Bureau of Archaeological Research in Tallahassee. The result is 8AL2500, which means this is the 2,500th site that has been recorded for Alachua County. Florida's site files are part of a national database.

Other Florida Rules and Regulations

People who hunt and fish in Florida know that there are restrictions on the season of the year that certain animals can be killed and also on their size, number, age, and even sex. Examples include redfish and deer, which are protected species. Rules and regulations are very strict with regard to endangered species, such as the manatee and the white pelican. Marine mammals, migratory birds, and birds of prey are protected whether they are endangered or not. These rules and regulations extend to the collection of dead animals, so if individuals wish to build their own comparative skeletal collection they should first familiarize themselves with current laws on the local, state, national, and international levels. Permission must be obtained from the proper authorities in order to avoid severe penalties.

The Florida Program of Vertebrate Paleontology protects and preserves vertebrate fossils and sites located on state-owned lands, including submerged lands. Permits to conduct field investigations are issued at the Florida Museum of Natural History, Gainesville, in accordance with Chapter 84–316, Laws of Florida, and the University of Florida Rule 6Cl-7.541 implementing this law. Fossil shark teeth, plants, and invertebrates, including shells, are excluded from the regulations.

CONCLUSION

After centuries of abuse and neglect of America's natural resources and cultural heritage, laws have been passed in an attempt to legislate an ethical behavior that values the protection of the collective wealth of our nation over free enterprise and rugged individualism. The subordination of personal gain to the national good is costly, complex, and restrictive, as is apparent from the descriptions of some of the rules and regulations given in the paragraphs above. Legislative changes are frequently made in an effort to plug loopholes spotted by persons and organizations not willing to abide by the laws. In some cases, people are oblivious to the rules or simply ignore them hoping they will not get caught. All in all, America's remaining environmental and cultural resources have a better chance of surviving into the future than they did a generation ago.

FLORIDA SITE FILE
GUIDELINES FOR USERS

November, 1993

Background State and federal law mandate that the state maintain an inventory of all known historic structures and archaeological sites. The Florida Site File, Bureau of Archaeological Research, Division of Historical Resources within the Department of State is the government office which maintains that inventory for Florida. About 81,000 sites (17,000 archaeological, 64,000 structural) are entered on the Site File as of November, 1993. These large numbers, however, represent only a small part of the heritage of Floridians, considering that less than 10% of the area of most Florida counties has seen field survey by qualified professionals such as archaeologists or architectural historians. Nearly 10,000 sites and over 300 reports on field surveys are added annually to the Site File.

Function The Site File is an archive and information source only; Site File staff evaluate neither the historical significance of sites nor the potential impact of development projects, although official and unofficial evaluations by others are sometimes included in our records. Consult the Compliance Review Section of the Bureau of Historic Preservation (904-487-2333) if you have inquiries related to preservation aspects of state project reviews, permits, or compliance procedures; inquiries related to local government comprehensive planning; or inquiries related to historical concerns on state lands.

Requesting Information Our staff assists researchers at our Tallahassee office and can sometimes perform limited research on request. Many, if not most, inquiries can be served with computer-printed county inventories as described below. Due to limited staff, research involving more than about fifteen minutes of staff time, including photocopying, will normally have to be done by the user. Charges may be made for resources used. In particular, we charge $0.15 per page for copying, although the charge may be waived for a small number of copies. Please consult with us well in advance of deadline, by letter or fax, not on the phone. Plan on a response time of two weeks for routine inquiries. Replies by fax or by express mail services will not ordinarily be possible, due to limited staff and equipment.

Locating Site or Survey Records Inquiries about sites should when possible refer to the state identification number which organizes all files. These numbers include a prefix of "8" for the state of Florida, a two letter county code, the number in assignment order within the county, and an optional terminal letter designating spatial or other subdivisions of the site. "8LE220" or "8LE00220", for example, refers to the 220th site recorded in Florida's Leon County. Historical structures are best searched by full street address and all known historical names; searches can be performed by legal survey location--township, range, and section--but this kind of search often lists many extraneous structures. Archaeological sites are best searched according to the map location on 1:24,000 topographic maps of the United States Geological Survey. Field survey searches are best performed when either the map location on FDOT county highway maps, or the county, report author, date, and report title are known.

6.2. Florida Site File Guidelines for Users, page 1.

Limiting the Distribution of Information As far as possible, we limit the distribution of location information on sites vulnerable to looting or vandalism, especially prehistoric archaeological sites and unprotected shipwrecks.

Using Standard County Inventories Many informational requests can be quickly satisfied from compact, one-line-per-site summaries of information printed from computer files. For all sites, these include site number, site name, National Register status, township-range-section location, and a code indicating the status of processing for the file. For historical structures, street address, city, and present use or function are also listed.   For archaeological sites, descriptive codes and a list of archaeological cultures occurring supplement the basic information.   When appropriate, information from Site File data bases can be furnished on computer media, for example, on diskettes.

Determining Site Eligibility The criteria for listing a property on the Florida Site File are that it be adequately documented and normally that it be at least 50 years old. Therefore entry of a property on the Site File does not necessarily imply that it is especially significant historically, although many listed properties have great significance.

Recording Sites Nonprofessionals have often furnished information useful in understanding and preserving historical sites. Two standard Site File forms are available for recording archaeological sites, one for professionals and one for amateurs. Another form is used for historical structures. Preliminary forms are available for recording historic shipwrecks, bridges, and cemeteries. These are required for entry of a site on the Site File. Supplementary documentation is normally required (site location on photostat of USGS topographic map for all sites; photograph and large scale street map for historical structures).

Large Number of Sites? Individuals or organizations with large numbers of sites to report may benefit from reporting in computer-readable modes instead of on paper forms: contact the Site File for details.

Documents Offering Further Information (single copies available on request)

Article in *Florida Anthropologist*, "The Florida Master Site File" (20 pp.)
Standard *Historical Structure Form* and manual for completing it (2 pp. on one sheet, 78 pp.)
Standard *Archaeological Site Form* and manual for completing it (2 pp. on one sheet, 90 pp.)
Archaeological Short Form for nonprofessionals (2pp. on one sheet; instructions on back of form)
County Inventories: Explanatory Handout with Example (6 pp.)

Address   Florida Site File
                                 Division of Historical Resources
                                 R. A. Gray Building, Room 425
                                 500 South Bronough Street
                                 Tallahassee, Florida 32399-0250
                                 Phone 904-487-2299 SUNCOM 277-2299; Fax 904-488-3353

6.2. Florida Site File Guidelines for Users, page 2.

SURVEY NO.*_____
Plottable?* Y_ N_

SURVEY LOG SHEET
FLORIDA MASTER SITE FILE
Version 1.1: 3/89

TITLE _____
_____

AUTHOR(S) _____
_____

ARCHAEOLOGIST/HISTORIAN _____
AFFILIATION _____
PUB. DATE _____ TOTAL NUMBER OF PAGES IN REPORT ____
PUBLICATION INFO _____
KEY WORDS/PHRASES DESCRIBING SURVEY* (max of 30 columns each)
_____
_____

REQUESTING GOVERNMENT UNIT, CORPORATION, OR PERSON
    NAME _____
    ADDRESS _____

DESCRIPTION OF SURVEY: NUMBER OF DISTINCT AREAS SURVEYED ____
    MONTH/YEAR DATES FOR FIELD WORK: START ___/___ THRU ___/___
    TOTAL AREA _____ac/ha IF CORRIDOR: WIDTH ___ft/m LENGTH ___mi/km
TYPE OF SURVEY (Use as many as apply): __archaeological
    __architectural __historical __underwater
    OTHER TYPE(S): _____

METHODS EMPLOYED (Use as many as apply): _unknown   _archival
    _pedestrian   _shovel test   _test excav. _posthole
    _extensive excav. _auger survey   _coring
    _remote sensing   _windshield   _surf.exposures
    OTHER METHOD(S) _____

SITES   Significance discussed? Y_ N_ Circle NR-elig/signif site nos:
OLD SITE NUMBERS : COUNT ____ LIST _____
_____
_____

NEW SITE NUMBERS : COUNT ____ LIST _____
_____

COUNTIES: _____
_____

USGS MAP(S)_____

TOWNSHIP/RANGE (list all township/range combinations eg, 04S/29E)
_____
_____

REMARKS (Use reverse if needed): _____
_____
_____
_____

SURVEY AREA MUST BE OUTLINED OR HIGHLIGHTED ON FDOT COUNTY HWY. MAP!
ATTACH OR PHOTOCOPY ONTO BACK OF FORM.

* For use of Fla. Master Site File only/Div. of Historical Resources/R. A. Gray Bldg/500 S. Bronough St/Tallahassee, FL 32399-0250

6.3. Survey Log Sheet.

ARCHAEOLOGICAL SITE FORM
FLORIDA SITE FILE
Version 2.1 5/94

Site #8 _____
Recorder # _____
Field Date ___/___/___
Form Date ___/___/___

SITE NAME(S) _____ [DIST #8 _____]
PROJECT NAME _____ [SURVEY # _____]
OWNERSHIP: ☐ private-profit ☐ private-nonprofit ☐ private-individ ☐ priv-unspecifd ☐ city ☐ county ☐ state ☐ federal ☐ unknown
USGS MAP NAME & DATE _____ COUNTY _____
TWP ___ RANGE ___ SECTION ___, ¼ Sect.: ☐ NE ☐ NW ☐ SE ☐ SW   IRREG. SECT.? ☐ y ☐ n
CITY/TOWN _____   IN CURRENT CITY LIMITS? ☐ y ☐ n
ADDRESS/VICINITY OF/ROUTE TO _____
_____
LANDGRANT _____ PARCEL # _____
NAME OF PUBLIC TRACT (e.g., park) _____

TYPE OF SITE (Check all choices that apply; if needed write others in at bottom)

SETTING	STRUCTURES OR FEATURES		FUNCTION	DENSITY
☐ land site	☐ aboriginal boat	☐ fort	☐ road segment	☐ none specified	☐ unknown
☐ _____	☐ agric/farm bldg	☐ midden	☐ shell midden	☐ campsite	☐ single artifact
☐ wetland fresh wtr	☐ burial mound	☐ mill unspecified	☐ shell mound	☐ extractive site	☐ diffuse scatter
☐ wetland salt/tidal	☐ building remains	☐ mission	☐ shipwreck	☐ habitatn/homestead	☐ dense scatter>2/m²
☐ undwtr (original)	☐ cemetery/grave	☐ mound unspecified	☐ subsurface features	☐ farmstead	☐ variable density
☐ undwtr (inundated)	☐ dump/refuse	☐ plantation	☐ surface scatter	☐ village/town	
☐ _____	☐ earthworks	☐ platform mound	☐ well	☐ quarry	

OTHER _____

HISTORIC CONTEXTS (Check all that apply, except use most specific subphases only)

ABORIGINAL					NONABORIGINAL
☐ Alachua	☐ Fort Walton	☐ Hickory Pond	☐ Perico Island	☐ Semi: Colonization	☐ 1st Spanish 1513-99
☐ Archaic unspecif	☐ Glades Ia	☐ Late Archaic	☐ Safety Harbor	☐ Semi: 1st War to 2d	☐ 1st Spanish 1600-99
☐ Belle Glade I	☐ Glades Ib	☐ Late Swift Creek	☐ St. Augustine	☐ Semi: 2d War to 3d	☐ 1st Spanish 1700-1763
☐ Belle Glade II	☐ Glades I unspec	☐ Leon-Jefferson	☐ St. Johns Ia	☐ Semi: 3d War on	☐ 1st Spanish unspecified
☐ Belle Glade III	☐ Glades IIa	☐ Malabar I	☐ St. Johns Ib	☐ Seminole-unspecif	☐ British 1763-1783
☐ Belle Glade IV	☐ Glades IIb	☐ Malabar II	☐ St. Johns I unspecif	☐ Swift Creek unspec	☐ 2d Spanish 1783-1821
☐ Belle Glade unspec	☐ Glades IIc	☐ Manasota	☐ St. Johns IIa	☐ Transitional	☐ Amer.Territor'l 1821-45
☐ Cades Pond	☐ Glades II unspec	☐ Middle Archaic	☐ St. Johns IIb	☐ Weeden Island I	☐ Amer.Civil War 1861-65
☐ Deptford	☐ Glades IIIa	☐ Mount Taylor	☐ St. Johns IIc	☐ Weeden Island II	☐ American 19th Century
☐ Early Archaic	☐ Glades IIIb	☐ Norwood	☐ St. Johns II unspecif	☐ Weeden Island unsp	☐ American 20th Century
☐ Early Swift Creek	☐ Glades IIIc	☐ Orange	☐ St. Johns unspecified	☐ prehistoric nonceram	☐ American unspecified
☐ Englewood	☐ Glades III unsp	☐ Paleo-Indian	☐ Santa Rosa	☐ prehistoric ceramic	☐ African-American
	☐ Glades unspecif	☐ Pensacola	☐ Santa Rosa-Swift Crk	☐ prehistoric unspecif	

OTHER (Less common phases are not checklisted. For historic sites also give specific dates if known) _____
_____

SURVEYOR'S EVALUATION OF SITE

Potentially elig. for local designation?   ☐ yes ☐ no ☐ insuff.info | Local Designation Category
Individually elig. for Nat. Register?   ☐ yes ☐ no ☐ insuff.info |
Potential contributor to NR district?   ☐ yes ☐ no ☐ insuff.info | _____

EXPLANATION OF EVALUATION (Required if evaluated; limit to 3 lines; attach full justification)
_____
_____

RECOMMENDATIONS FOR SITE _____
_____

DHR USE ONLY======== OFFICIAL EVALUATIONS ========DHR USE ONLY
NR DATE	KEEPER-NR ELIGIBILITY: ☐ y ☐ n ☐ pe ☐ ii Date ___/___/____
___/___/____	SHPO-NR ELIGIBILITY: ☐ y ☐ n ☐ pe ☐ ii Date ___/___/____
DELIST DATE	LOCAL DESIGNATION: _____ Date ___/___/____
___/___/____	Local office _____

HR6E04506-92 Florida Site File/Division of Historical Resources/Gray Bldg/500 S Bronough/Tallahassee FL 32399-0250/904-487-2299/Suncom 277-2299

Computer Document File Irving F:\FORMS\AR_REV21.DOC

6.4. Archaeological Site Form, page 1.

ARCHAEOLOGICAL SITE FORM
Division of Historical Resources, Florida Department of State

FIELD METHODS (Check one or more methods for detection and for boundaries)

SITE DETECTION

☐ no field check   ☐ exposed ground   ☐ screened shovel

☐ literature search   ☐ posthole digger   _____

☐ informant report   ☐ auger--size:___   _____

☐ remote sensing   ☐ unscreend shovel   _____

Number, size, depth, pattern of units; screen size _____

SITE BOUNDARIES

☐ bounds unknown   ☐ remote sensing   ☐ unscreened shovel

☐ none by recorder   ☐ insp exposed ground   ☐ screened shovel

☐ literature search   ☐ posthole digger   ☐ block excavations

☐ informant report   ☐ auger--size:___   ☐ estimate or guess

SITE DESCRIPTION

EXTENT Size (m²) _____ Depth/stratigraphy of cultural deposit _____

TEMPORAL INTERPRETATION Components: ☐ single ☐ prob single ☐ prob multiple ☐ multiple ☐ uncertain

Describe each occupation in plan (refer to attached large scale map) and stratigraphically. Discuss temporal and functional interpretations.

_____

_____

INTEGRITY Overall disturbance: ☐ none seen ☐ minor ☐ substantial ☐ major ☐ redeposited ☐ destroyed-document!

Disturbances/threats/protective measures _____

AREA COLLECTED _____ m² Surface: #collect. units _____ . Excavation: #contig. blks _____

ARTIFACTS

TOTAL ARTIFACTS #____ (C)ount or (E)stimate? __ Surface #_____ Subsurface # _____

COLLECTION STRATEGY

☐ unknown   ☐ unselective (all artifacts)

         ☐ selective (some artifacts)

☐ uncollected   ☐ general (not by subarea)

         ☐ controlled (by subarea)

ARTIFACT/FEATURE CATEGORIES

☐ unspecified   ☐ daub   ☐ nonlocal-exotic   ☐ bone-unspecif

☐ lithics, aborig'l   ☐ brick/bldg matl   ☐ metal, nonprecious   ☐ unworked shell

☐ ceramic-aborig'l   ☐ glass   ☐ bone-human   ☐ worked shell

☐ ceramic-nonabo   ☐ precious metal/coin   ☐ bone-animal   ☐ subsurf feats

Other (Strategy, Categories)_____

DIAGNOSTICS (Type and frequency)

1_____ N=__   6_____ N=__

2_____ N=__   7_____ N=__

3_____ N=__   8_____ N=__

4_____ N=__   9_____ N=__

5_____ N=__   10_____ N=__

     11_____ N=__

ENVIRONMENT

Nearest fresh water (incl. relic source) _____ Dist. (m/ft)/bearing _____

Natural community_____

Local vegetation _____

Topography _____ Elevation_____m/ft

Present land use _____

SCS soil series _____ Soil association _____

FURTHER INFORMATION

INFORMANT(S): Name/Addr./Phone_____

LOCATION & FILE NOS. (Field notes, artifacts/accession nos, photographs/negative nos.)

_____

MANUSCRIPTS OR PUBLICATIONS ON THE SITE (Use Continuation Sheet, give FSF# if relevant)

RECORDER(S): Name/Addr./Phone _____

     Affiliation or FAS Chapter_____

LARGE SCALE MAP: At 1"=200' or larger scale, show: site boundaries, scale, North arrow, datum, test/collection units, landmarks.

NARRATIVE DESCRIPTION/CONTINUATIONS: Attach additional sheets with detailed information or with continuations.

6.4. Archaeological Site Form, page 2.

HISTORICAL STRUCTURE FORM
FLORIDA SITE FILE
Version 2.1 5/94

Site #8 _____
Recorder # _____
Field Date __/__/__
Form Date __/__/__

☐ Original
☐ Update

SITE NAMES (addr. if none) _____ [MULT. LIST. #8 _____]
SURVEY _____ [SURVEY # _____]
NATIONAL REGISTER CATEGORY   ☐ building   ☐ structure   ☐ district   ☐ site   ☐ object

LOCATION & IDENTIFICATION

ADDRESS (Include N,S,E,W; st., ave., etc.) _____
CROSS STREETS nearest/between _____
CITY/TOWN _____ IN CURRENT CITY LIMITS __yes __no
COUNTY _____ TAX PARCEL # _____
SUBDIVISION NAME _____ BLOCK _____ LOT NO. _____
OWNERSHIP ☐ private-profit ☐ priv-nonprofit ☐ priv-indiv ☐ priv-unspecified ☐ city ☐ county ☐ state ☐ federal ☐ unknown
NAME OF PUBLIC TRACT (e.g., park) _____
ROUTE TO _____

MAPPING

USGS 7.5' MAP NAME _____
TOWNSHIP ____ RANGE ____ SECT. ____ 1/4 ____ IRREG. SECT.? ☐ y   ☐ n
PLAT OR OTHER MAP (Map's name, location) _____
LANDGRANT _____

DESCRIPTION

STYLE _____ EXTERIOR PLAN _____ NO. STORIES ____
STRUCTURAL SYSTEMS _____
FOUNDATION: Types _____ Materials _____
EXTERIOR FABRICS _____
ROOF: Types _____ Materials _____
  Secondary strucs. (dormers etc.) _____
CHIMNEY : No. ___ Materials _____ LOCATIONS _____
WINDOWS (types, materials, etc.) _____

MAIN ENTRANCE (stylistic details) _____
PORCHES: #open ____ #closed ____ #incised ____ Locations _____
  Porch roof types _____
EXTERIOR ORNAMENT _____

INTERIOR PLAN _____ CONDITION: ☐ excellent ☐ good ☐ fair ☐ deteriorated ☐ ruinous
SURROUNDINGS (N-None, S-Some, M-Most, A-All/nearly all) ☐ commercial ☐ residential ☐ institutional ☐ rural
ANCILLARY FEATURES (No., type of outbuildings; major landscape features) _____

ARCHAEOLOGICAL REMAINS _____
NARRATIVE (Use Continuation sheet. E.g. description of interior, landscape, architecture, etc)

CROSS-REFERENCES

BIBLIOGRAPHIC REFERENCES (Use Continuation Sheet, give FSF Manuscript # If relevant) __
PHOTOGRAPHS (REQUIRED) B&W print(s) at least 3 x 5, at least one main facade.
Location of negatives/neg. nos. _____

HR6E04606-92 Florida Site File, Div. of Historical Resources,Gray Bldg,500 S Bronough,Tallahassee, FL 32399-0250/904-487-2299/Suncom 277-2299
Computer File Irving F:\FORMS\strucfm2.doc

6.5. Historical Structure Form, page 1.

HISTORICAL STRUCTURE FORM

HISTORY

CONSTRUCTION DATE _____ CIRCA ☐ yes ☐ no
ARCHITECT: (last name first) _____
BUILDER: (last name first) _____
MOVES   ☐ yes ☐ no   Dates _____   Orig.addr. _____
ALTERATIONS ☐ yes ☐ no   Dates _____   Nature _____
ADDITIONS   ☐ yes ☐ no   Dates _____   Nature _____
ORIGINAL USES (give dates)_____
INTERMEDIATE USES (give dates) _____
PRESENT USES (give dates) _____
OWNERSHIP HISTORY (especially original owner) _____
_____
_____

SURVEYOR'S EVALUATION OF SITE

				Local Designation Category
Potentially elig. for local designation?	☐ yes	☐ no	☐ insuff. info	
Individually elig. for Nat. Register?	☐ yes	☐ no	☐ insuff. info	_____
Potential contributor to NR district?	☐ yes	☐ no	☐ insuff. info	_____

HISTORICAL ASSOCIATIONS (ethnic heritage, etc.) _____
_____
_____

EXPLANATION OF EVALUATION (required; limit to three lines; attach full statement on separate sheet)
_____
_____
_____
_____

RESEARCH METHODS (Check all choices that apply; if needed write others at bottom)

☐ arch'l survey/testing	☐ Sanborn maps	☐ building permits	☐ occupation permits
☐ exposures inspected	☐ FSF survey search	☐ demolition permits	☐ FL Photo Archives
☐ controlled arch'l surf coll	☐ FSF sites search	☐ commercial permits	☐ arch'l form completed
☐ occupant interview	☐ FL Archives	☐ plat maps	☐ not applicable
☐ neighbor interview	☐ newspapers	☐ subdivision map	
☐ tax records/property deeds	☐ library research-local	☐ interior inspection	
☐ tax records only	☐ lib. special collections	☐ public lands survey	
☐ other methods (specify) _____			

RECORDER

NAME (last first)/ADDR/PHONE/AFFILIATION _____
_____

DHR USE ONLY====== OFFICIAL EVALUATIONS ======DHR USE ONLY
NR DATE   KEEPER-NR ELIGIBILITY*: ☐ y ☐ n ☐ pe ☐ ii Date ___/___/___
___/___   SHPO-NR ELIGIBILITY*:   ☐ y ☐ n ☐ pe ☐ ii Date ___/___/___
DELIST DATE   LOCAL DESIGNATION*: _____ Date ___/___/___
___/___   Local office _____

REQUIRED: (1) USGS MAP WITH STRUCTURE PINPOINTED
             (2) LARGE SCALE STREET OR PLAT MAP
             (3) PHOTO OF MAIN FACADE, PREFER B&W, AT LEAST 3X5

6.5. Historical Structure Form, page 2.

SUPPLEMENT FOR SITE FORMS

Site # _____

SITE NAME _____

NATURE OF SITE __standing structure __archaeological site __both

A. NARRATIVE DESCRIPTION OF SITE (Use back and continuations if necessary)

B. DISCUSSION OF SIGNIFICANCE (Use back of page and continuations)

C. HISTORY AND BIBLIOGRAPHY OF PAST WORK AT SITE (Use back and continuation sheets)

Fla. Site File, Div. of Hist. Resources,Gray Bldg,500 S Bronough,Tallahassee. FL 32399-0250/904-487-2299/Suncom 277-2299

FDHR Form HR6E64706-92   Computer Document Zelda C:\FORMS\SUPPFM.DOC

6.6. Supplement for Historical Structure and Archaeological Site forms.

AFTERWORD

An invisible cultural heritage lies buried beneath your feet. Silent until accidentally or intentionally exposed, its real story will be told only if recorded accurately. In this book I have attempted to explain why the responsibility for the recovery, identification, classification, and interpretation of information about the world's ancient peoples and their activities should reside within the profession of archaeology. Conclusions about chronological, geographical, and cultural boundaries must be deduced by the archaeologist without the benefit of written records and with only the small percentage of material items (artifacts) that survive the ravages of time. Given these restrictions, archaeologists have continuously made use of new or refined techniques, including space age instrumentation, to enhance their ability to repeople the landscapes of bygone times. The most critical ingredients, however, are an understanding of anthropological theory and a knowledge of the world's past and present preindustrial people. The archaeologist does not expect to recognize departed heroes or identify many major events, but day-by-day activities crystallize as pieces of the puzzle are fitted together.

Using Florida as a case study throughout, I summarized in the first chapter what is known about the state's early inhabitants based on knowledge that began to accumulate approximately 150 years ago and increases daily. In the second chapter, I described how data gathering is accomplished through systematic survey and excavation, pointing out that most archaeological fieldwork had its roots in nineteenth-century antiquarianism (collecting artifacts unscientifically). These very collections, however, made it possible to establish typologies that have become the framework upon which questions can be asked and problems investigated. The following three chapters (on analysis, dating, and preservation) detail how the expertise and technology of many disciplines benefit the archaeological profession. The evidence furnished by these specialties becomes part of the data base used by the archaeologist to piece together information about resources, settlement patterns, activities, and even the belief systems utilized by the people being studied. The final chapter describes rules and regulations, particularly those that pertain to the protection of America's cultural heritage, that have emerged to curb the loss of information resulting from the pothunter's shovel and the developer's backhoe.

As fields of interest develop, expand, and diversify through time, mistakes in method and interpretation are often made. Examples from all of the sciences can be cited, and archaeology is no exception. Fortunately, it is possible to learn from mistakes. The gravest errors in archaeology were made in the ways that data were collected in the field with little regard for stratigraphic sequences. By simply digging holes, it is virtually impossible to establish relative dates for materials that are recovered or to recognize how they are associated with other objects or structures. This is the approach used by the antiquarian. A primary goal of this book is to turn the reader away from antiquarianism.

I mentioned in the preface that archaeology is seldom exciting. Does this mean that most archaeologists wish they had chosen another profession? I believe the answer to that question is an unqualified NO! It is always exciting to learn something new about something old.

GLOSSARY OF TERMS

The language of archaeology and anthropology sometimes uses familiar words in a specific way. The following words or phrases are defined according to these particular meanings.

Absolute dating: The determination of age with reference to a fixed time scale; also called chronometric dating.

Acculturation: The process and results of borrowing or adopting the cultural traits and social patterns of another group.

Aplastics: Intentional or accidental inclusions in pottery clays before firing; temper.

Archaic: Usually refers to a time period in North America from about 9000 to 4000 B.P.; also refers to a seminomadic way of life.

Assemblage: A group of artifacts recurring together at a particular time and place.

Assimilation: The merging of cultural traits from previously distinct cultural groups. When an individual or group become thoroughly immersed into a new culture so that they cannot be distinguished from it.

Atlatl: A stick fitted with a handle on one end and a groove at the other used to increase the velocity and force in throwing a spear; a spearthrower.

Badge of office/identity: Clothing, crowns, tatoos, head deformation, social attitudes, or even language that become established to set certain individuals apart from others in society.

Balk: The wall of an excavation unit that is left standing to preserve the stratification so that it can be recorded and mapped.

Bearings: A direction or relative position; a horizontal direction expressed in degrees east or west of a true or magnetic north or south direction.

Black drink: Made from the roasted leaves of cassina *(Ilex vomitoria)*, it was used in the Southeast as a sacred tea and an everyday beverage because of its caffeine content.

Bola stone: A stone object usually associated with the Paleoindian period in Florida; about the size and shape of a hen's egg with a shallow indentation at the smaller end.

Botanical material: Plants.

Calcium carbonate: $CaCO_3$; a major constituent of limestone, shell, and bone.

Calendric: Assigned a specific date—usually day, month, year—but also used sometimes to describe a date received by radiocarbon analysis or some other chronometric technique.

Catchment area/basin: Area of potential or actual resources exploited by a group, usually occurring within easy walking distance of a settlement.

Central places: Primary centers or settlements surrounded by secondary satellite communities.

Ceramics: Fired clay objects.

Chert: *See* flint.

Chipped stone: The method and the result of producing artifacts of flint (chert) by percussion and pressure as compared to polished stone objects, which are manufactured in a different way.

Chronological position: The relative or absolute age of a deposit or artifact; younger or older than other deposits or artifacts.

Chronometric dating: *See* absolute dating.

Classification: An arbitrary means to place all phenomena into orderly categories so they can be assessed systematically.

Clay balls: Lumps of fired clay. In Florida they appear in deposits predating pottery bowls.

Contact period: A.D. 1492 in the Americas; usually considered A.D. 1513 with the arrival of Ponce de León in Florida.

Context: A description of the horizontal and vertical position of an artifact, its associated materials, and surrounding matrix.

Coprolite: Preserved fecal material; when analyzed, a valuable source of information about diet.

Cost-effective: Economical, considering time and energy spent procuring specific resources compared to the real benefits derived from the resources.

Cranium: Skull; the part of the skull that encloses the brain.

Crystalline: Rocks and minerals having a regular molecular structure as compared to amorphous materials like glass or obsidian.

Cultigen: A plant showing some evidence of having been protected or modified by human intervention as opposed to a cultivar that is produced under cultivation.

Culture area: An arbitrary geographic or research area in which general cultural homogeneity is found.

Curation: Preservation and protection of collections and structures for the future.

Data universe: A defined area of archaeological investigation, bounded in time and space, often a geographic region or an archaeological site (from Fagan 1991).

Datum plane: A point of reference from which all vertical measurements (elevations) are made; can be arbitrary or calculated from height above sea level.

Datum point: A location, usually tied into a permanent U.S. Geologic Survey bench mark, from which all measurements are made.

Debitage: By-products or refuse resulting from the manufacture of objects from a raw material, such as stone.

Deposition: Refers to the natural and cultural accumulation of materials and sediments that makes it possible to define stratigraphic sequences often having chronological significance.

Direct percussion: A method utilized to produce chipped stone implements; flint (chert) material is struck with a rock or antler hammer resulting in the removal of flakes, which reduces the stone to the desirable size and shape.

Division of labor: How tasks are assigned among members of a group; can be based on sex (men's tasks, women's tasks), age, or speciality.

Early Historic period: In Florida, from the time of Ponce de León in 1513 to approximately the mid-1700s.

Ecofacts: Materials recovered at archaeological sites that may have been deposited as a result of human activity but that are not artifacts, such as bones, plants, sediments, etc.

Ecology: The study of the relationships between organisms and their environment.

Erosion: Alteration or obliteration of a deposit or surface.

Ethnocentrism: Believing or acting as if the ways of your people are superior to those of other people.

Ethnography: A description of how people of another culture live.

Eutectic development: The lowest melting temperature obtainable with mixtures of given components that do not form solid solutions.

Fauna: Animals.

Flakes: Usually refers to pieces of chert (flint) that have been intentionally struck from a nodule and bear certain typical characteristics such as a striking platform and bulb of percussion.

Flint: Also chert. Stone material that fractures in a patterned, predictable way because of its randomly oriented microcrystalline or cryptocrystalline structure of SiO_2.

Flora: Plants.

Formative stage: Cultures having the presence of agriculture or any other subsistence economy of comparable effectiveness; the successful integration of such an economy into well-established, sedentary village life.

Fossil: The remains of plants or animals that have been preserved by being turned to stone by the gradual replacement of their tissues with infiltrated mineral matter; fossilization or petrification.

Friable: Easily crumbled.

Hardpan: A hard impervious layer that prevents the downward movement of water and roots.

Homogeneous: Composed of parts that are equal or essentially alike.

Hydrate: Formed by the union of water with some other substance.

Inorganic: Materials, such as rocks and minerals, that are not animals or plants.

In situ: Occurring in its natural position or place.

Inundate: Flood.

Kill hole: Hole made in an object by ceremonial mutilation or breakage, when the object is placed with a body at time of burial.

Knap: To produce stone tools by striking flakes from a core or nodule of flint.

Lithic technology: The study and replication of stone implements to gain insight into methods used and problems solved by people in the past.

Matrilineal clans: Relationships reckoned by descent through the female line.

Matrix: A natural deposit in which objects become embedded.

Microcrystals: A rock in which the individual crystals can be seen only through a microscope.

Multicomponent: The presence of more than one cultural phase at a site.

Nonprobabilistic sampling: Sampling using instinctual criteria such as an archaeologist's experience.

Organic: Plant and animal materials.

Paleoindian: A time period in American archaeology from about 11,500 to 10,000 B.P.; a way of life based on big game hunting of now extinct Pleistocene megafauna.

Palynology: The study of past vegetation and climate through pollen records.

Patinated: A weathered layer; usually refers to a measurable thickness on the outer surface of a flint artifact when viewed in a freshly broken cross section.

Pedestaled: Features or burials that extend into a lower level that are left in place (on a pedestal) until fully exposed as excavation proceeds around them.

Planview: To view or draw an excavation unit or site by looking straight down on it; a horizontal section.

Pollen: The fertilizing element of flowering plants; a male gamete or sexual cell.

Pothunter: An individual who ravages archaeological sites to collect only items of value or beauty like whole pots, spearheads, carvings; an antiquarian.

Potlid fracture: Occurs when flint material is heated too rapidly.

Preform: In flint working, the term refers to a stage of biface (spearhead or arrowhead) manufacture that exhibits the maintenance of symmetry and balance during the reduction process.

Prehistory: In the Americas, the time prior to A.D. 1492.

Pressure flaking: In flint working, the removal of flakes by pressing them from the edge of a nearly finished spearhead using the tip of a hard sharp material such as deer tine, tooth, or copper.

Primary burial: Usually a flexed or extended burial.

Probabilistic sampling: Sampling based on statistical criteria and probability theory.

Profile: The vertical face exposed during excavations that shows the stratigraphy (as opposed to planview).

Protohistoric: In North America, a time period before actual contact when it is apparent that some impact has occurred; often refers to the presence among Indian groups of diseases or trade items that have been transmitted prior to face-to-face encounters.

Provenience: The three-dimensional location of an artifact or feature in an excavation unit.

Pyrotechniques: The application and control of elevated temperatures to bring about changes in raw materials.

Relative dating: Establishing a chronological sequence without reference to an absolute time scale; based on the Law of Superposition and the assumption that a specimen is younger or older depending on its position in the profile.

Seasonality studies: Determining the time of year that a site was occupied based on certain plant or animal remains. For example, hickory nuts indicate a late summer-fall occupation.

Seasoned: To mature or age by exposure to certain conditions or treatment; as with wood or bone, a material that works better if it is not used immediately after it is cut or killed.

Secondary burial: Indicates that after death a human body has been placed in a charnel house until the flesh decays and the bones are cremated, or disarticulated and bundled, before being buried in the ground.

Sediments: Soils.

Seminoles: The name given to Indian groups who migrated to Florida after most of the original Florida Indians were exterminated. The Seminoles now reside on land set aside for them in South Florida and Oklahoma.

Seriation: A method to establish chronology where culture sequences and dates are not known. Based on changes that occur in artifact types (from Jennings 1989).

Sexagesimal system: Based on the number sixty; a fraction whose denominator is sixty or a power of sixty.

Sherds: Pieces or fragments of broken ceramics.

Single component: The manifestation of a specific time period at a site.

Spearthrower: *See* atlatl.

Species: The basic category of biological classification; closely related plants or animals capable of interbreeding.

Spoil piles: Soil and other materials that accumulate as a result of excavations at an archaeological site. Spoil piles (back dirt) are used to refill the units when excavations are completed.

Stage: A way of life, such as the big game hunting stage of the Paleoindian period.

Staples: The food products most depended upon for survival.

Strata: Layers seen in the vertical face of an excavation unit; can be natural or cultural and may have chronological significance. Singular: stratum.

Stratigraphy: A study of strata.

Taphonomy: The study of the processes that transform organic materials after deposition.

Taxonomy: The science dealing with classification.

Technology: The application of science.

Tempers: In pottery making, the constituents added to clay materials prior to firing.

Three-dimensional: In archaeology, refers to the north-south, east-west, and vertical (elevation) coordinates of an object, feature, level, etc. (one vertical and two horizontal measurements).

Topography: Relief features or surface configurations of a region or site.

Travois: A primitive vehicle used for hauling objects, consisting of two poles mounted on either side of a dog or horse and trailing on the ground, bearing a platform or net to hold the load.

Type: In archaeology, a particular artifact style (for example, a Clovis point) in which several attributes combine or cluster with sufficient frequency or in such distinctive ways that it can be recognized when seen again.

Typology: Systematic classification of phenomena based on shared attributes.

Unifacial: Worked only on one side or face, as opposed to bifacial.

Weathering: The process whereby materials are altered through time; can occur slowly or rapidly depending upon the composition of the objects, the environment in which they are buried, and changes in the environment.

BIBLIOGRAPHY

REFERENCES CITED

Arnold, J. R., and W. F. Libby

1949 Age Determination by Radiocarbon Context. Checks with Samples of Known Age. *Science* 110:678–80.

Bennett, Charles E.

1968 *Settlement of Florida*. Gainesville: University Presses of Florida.

1975 *Three Voyages by René Laudonniere*. Gainesville: University Presses of Florida.

Bond, F. Bligh

1918 *The Gate of Remembrance*. New York: E. P. Dutton.

Bullen, Ripley P.

1959 The Transitional Period of Florida. *Southeastern Archaeological Conference Newsletter* 6:43–53, 59–62.

Bullen, Ripley P., and J.B. Stoltman, eds.

1972 *Fiber-tempered Pottery in Southeastern United States and Northern Columbia: Its Origins, Context, and Significance*. Florida Anthropological Society Publications 6.

Cordell, Ann S.

1984 *Ceramic Technology at a Weeden Island Period Archaeological Site in North Florida*. Ceramic Notes No. 2. Occasional Publications of the Ceramic Technology Laboratory, Gainesville: Florida State Museum.

Cushing, Frank Hamilton

1897 Exploration of Ancient Key Dwellers' Remains on the Gulf Coast of Florida. *Proceedings of the American Philosophical Society* 25(153):329–448.

Daniel, I. Randolph, Jr., and Michael Wisenbaker

1987 *Harney Flats: A Florida Paleo-Indian Site.* Farmingdale, N.Y.: Baywood.

Doran, Glen H., and David N. Dickel

1988 Multidisciplinary Investigations at the Windover Site. In *Wet Site Archaeology,* edited by Barbara A. Purdy, pp. 263–89. West Caldwell, N.J.: Telford Press.

Fagan, Brian M.

1991 *In the Beginning.* 7th ed. New York: Harper Collins.

Gilliland, Marion Spjut

1975 *The Material Culture of Key Marco, Florida.* Gainesville: University Presses of Florida.

Goggin, John M.

1949 The Archaeology of the Glades Area, Southern Florida. Manuscript on file at Yale Peabody Museum.

Goodyear, Albert C.

1969 A Deptford Vessel from Pinellas County, Florida. *Florida Anthropologist* 22(1–4):34–35.

Granberry, Julian

1971 Final Collation of Texts, Vocabulary Lists, Grammar, of Timucua for Publication. *The American Philosophical Society Year Book* 1970 (1 January–31 December): 606–7.

Griffin, John W.

1988 *The Archeology of the Everglades National Park: A Synthesis.* Tallahassee: National Park Service, Southeast Archaeological Center.

Haynes, C. Vance, Jr.

1982 Were Clovis Progenitors in Beringia? In *Paleoecology of Beringia,* edited by David M. Hopkins, John V. Matthews, Jr., Charles E. Schweger, and Steven B. Young, pp. 383–98. New York: Academic Press.

Heizer, Robert F.

1966 *A Guide to Archaeological Field Methods.* 3d rev. ed. 1949. Palo Alto, Calif.: National Press.

Jennings, Jesse D.

1989 *Prehistory of North America.* Mountain View, Calif.: Mayfield.

Kohler, Timothy

1978 The Social and Chronological Dimensions of Village Occupation at a North Florida Weeden Island Site. Ph.D. diss., Department of Anthropology, University of Florida, Gainesville.

Lanning, John T.

1935 The Spanish Missions of Georgia. Chapel Hill: University of North Carolina Press.

Leader, Jonathan

    1985 Metal Artifacts from Fort Center: Aboriginal Metal Working in the Southeastern United States. Master's thesis, Department of Anthropology, University of Florida, Gainesville.

    1988 Technological Continuities and Specialization in Prehistoric Metalwork in the Eastern United States. Ph.D. diss., Department of Anthropology, University of Florida, Gainesville.

McGee, Ray M., and Ryan J. Wheeler

    1994 Stratigraphic Excavations at Groves Orange Midden, Lake Monroe, Volusia County, Florida: Methodology and Results. *Florida Anthropologist* 47(4):333–49.

Michell, John.

    1983 The New View over Atlantis. San Francisco: Harper and Row.

Milanich, Jerald T.

    1994 *Archaeology of Precolumbian Florida.* Gainesville: University Press of Florida.

Milanich, Jerald T., ed.

    1984 *McKeithen Weeden Island: The Culture of Northern Florida A.D. 200–900.* New York: Academic Press.

Mitchem, Jeffrey M., and Jonathan M. Leader

    1988 Early Sixteenth Century Beads from the Tatham Mound, Citrus County, Florida: Data and Interpretations. *Florida Anthropologist* 41(1):42–60.

Moore, Clarence B.

    1894 Certain Sand Mounds of the St. John's River, Florida, Part II. *Journal of the Academy of Natural Sciences of Philadelophia,* 2d series, 10.

    1900 Certain Antiquities of the Florida West-Coast. *Journal of the Academy of Natural Sciences of Philadelphia* 11:349–94.

    1921 Notes on the Shell Implements from Florida. *American Anthropologist* (n.s.) 23(1):12–18.

Moore, C.B., J.D. McGuire, F.W. Putnam, George A. Dorsey, Warren K. Moorehead, and Charles C. Willoughby

    1903 Discussion as to Copper from the Mounds. *American Anthropologist* 5(1): 27–57.

Morgan, William N,

    1980 *Prehistoric Architecture in the Eastern United States.* Cambridge; MIT Press.

Morris, Donald H.

    1975 Warm Mineral Springs Man. Manuscript on file, Division of Historical Research, Department of State. Tallahassee.

Newsom, Lee A.

    1987 Analysis of Botanical Remains from Hontoon Island (8-VO-202), Florida: 1980–1985 Excavations. *Florida Anthropologist* 40(1):47–84.

Prentice, Guy

1983 An Experiment in Shellworking. Manuscript prepared for lithic technology course, in the possession of Barbara A. Purdy.

Purdy, Barbara A.

1981 *Florida's Prehistoric Stone Technology*. Gainesville: University Presses of Florida.

1991 *The Art and Archaeology of Florida's Wetlands*. Boca Raton, Fla.: CRC Press.

Purdy, Barbara A., and H. K. Brooks

1971 Thermal Alteration of Silica Materials: An Archaeological Approach. *Science* 173:322–25.

Reiger, John F.

1979 The Making of Aboriginal Shell Tools: Clues from South Florida. *Florida Anthropologist* 32(4):130–38.

1981 An Analysis of Four Types of Shell Artifacts from South Florida. *Florida Anthropologist* 34(1):4–20.

Reitz, Elizabeth J., and C. Margaret Scarry

1985 *Reconstructing Historic Subsistence with an Example from Sixteenth-Century Spanish Florida*. The Society for Historical Archaeology, Special Publication Series, 3.

Renfrew, Colin and Paul Bahn

1991 *Archaeology*. New York: Thames and Hudson.

Scarry, C. Margaret

1985 Paleoethnobotany of the Granada Site. In *Archaeology and History of the Granada Site, Vol. I: Excavations at the Granada Site,* pp. 181–248. Tallahassee: Division of Archives, History, and Records Management.

Sears, William H.

1982 *Fort Center: An Archaeological Site in the Lake Okeechobee Basin*. Gainesville: University Presses of Florida

Shepard, Anna O.

1976 *Ceramics for the Archaeologist*. Carnegie Institution of Washington, Publication 609.

Smith, Marion

1989 Guide to the Archaeological Site Form of the Florida Master Site File. *Florida Archaeological Reports* 8. Tallahassee: Bureau of Archaeological Research, Division of Historical Resources.

Smith, Marion, and R. Douglas Walton, Jr.

1989 The Florida Master Site File. *Florida Anthropologist* 42(1):57–76.

Solis de Merás

1964 *Pedro Menéndez de Avilés* . Translated by J.T. Connor. Gainesville: University Presses of Florida.

Stuiver, Minze, and Bernd Becker

1986 High-Precision Decadal Calibration of the Radiocarbon Time Scale, A.D. 1950–2500 B.C. *Radiocarbon* 28(2B):863–910.

Swanton, John R.

1946 The Indians of the Southeastern United States. *Bureau of American Ethnology Bulletin* 137. Washington, D.C.: Smithsonian Institution.

Taylor, W.W.

1948 A Study of Archaeology. *American Anthropological Association Memoir* 69.

Tesar, Louis B.

1990 *The Historic Preservation Compliance Review Program of the Florida Department of State.* Tallahassee: Division of Historical Resources.

True, David O., ed.

1944 *Memoir of D$^{O.}$ d'Escalante Fontaneda Respecting Florida.* Translated by. Buckingham Smith. 1854. Reprint, with revisions, Coral Gables, Fla.: University of Miami Press.

Webb, S. D.

1994 Personal communication.

Webb, S. D., Jerald T. Milanich, Roger Alexon, and James S. Dunbar

1984 A *Bison antiquus* Kill Site, Wacissa River, Taylor County, Florida. *American Antiquity* 49:384–92.

Webster, William J.

1970 A New Concept for the *Busycon* Shell Receptacle. *Florida Anthropologist* 23(1):1–7.

Willey, Gordon R.

1949a *Excavations in Southeast Florida.* Yale University Publications in Anthropology 42.

1949b *Archaeology of the Florida Gulf Coast.* Smithsonian Miscellaneous Collections 113. Washington, D.C.: Smithsonian Institution.

1985 Comments on the Archaeology of Northwest Florida in 1984. Part 2. *Florida Anthropologist* 38(1–2):178–83.

Wing, Elizabeth S., and L. Jill Loucks

1985 Granada Site Faunal Analysis. In *Excavations at the Granada Site,* edited by John W. Griffin, pp. 259–346. Tallahassee: Division of Archives, History, and Records Management.

RECOMMENDED READING

Allerton, David, George M. Luer, and Robert S. Carr

1984 Ceremonial Tablets and Related Objects from Florida. *Florida Anthropologist* 37(1):5–54.

Andrews, E.W., and C.M. Andrews, eds.

1945 *Jonathan Dickinson's Journal or, God's Protecting Providence.* 1699. Reprint, New Haven: Yale University Press.

Benson, Elizabeth P., ed.

1977 *The Sea in the Pre-Columbian World.* Washington, D.C.: Dumbarton Oaks Research Library and Collections.

Bullen, Ripley P.

1975 *A Guide to the Identification of Florida Projectile Points.* Gainesville: Kendall Books.

Goggin, John M.

1952 *Space and Time Perspectives in Northern St. Johns Archeology, Florida.* Yale University Publications in Anthropology 47.

Griffin, John W., Sue B. Richardson, Mary Pohl, Carl D. McMurray, C. Margaret Scarry, Suzanne K. Fish, Elizabeth S. Wing, L. Jill Loucks, and Marcia K. Welch

1982 *Excavations at the Granada Site: Archaeology and History of the Granada Site.* Vol. 1. Tallahassee: Florida Division of Archives, History, and Records Management.

Joukowsky, M.

1981 *Complete Manual of Field Archaeology.* Englewood Cliffs, N.J.: Prentice Hall.

Lyon, Eugene

1976 The Enterprise of Florida: Pedro Menéndez de Avilés and the Spanish Conquest of 1565–1568. Gainesville: University of Florida Press.

Milanich, Jerald T., and Charles H. Fairbanks

1980 *Florida Archaeology.* New York: Academic Press.

Milanich, Jerald T., and Susan Milbrath, eds.

1989 *First Encounters.* Gainesville: University Presses of Florida.

Milanich, Jerald T. and Samuel Proctor, eds.

1978 *Tacachale.* Gainesville: University Presses of Florida.

Purdy, Barbara A., ed.

1988 *Wetsite Archaeology.* West Caldwell, N.J.: Telford Press.

Rouse, Irving

1951 *A Survey of Indian River Archeology, Florida.* Yale University Publications in Anthropology 44.

Smith, Hale G.

1956 *The European and the Indian, European-Indian Contacts in Georgia and Florida.* Florida Anthropological Society Publications 4.

INDEX

Page numbers in italics denote illustrations.

Artifacts: classifying, 2; definition, 2; diagnostic artifacts, 15, 37; European influence on, 69; labeling, 99-100; locating on grid, 91-92; nondiagnostic, 11; non-native, 2; provenience of, 23; recording location of, in grid, 91, *91;* recording of, 91; screening, 100-101; sorting, 100-101; type, 2

Atlatl (spearthrower): Eastern Woodlands, 13; hooks, *13;* as technological advance, 13

Aucilla River, 5

Auto-Ranger instrument, 88

Backdirt, 94, 105

Badges of identity, 67, *67*

Balks, 96-98; McKeithen Island, *97*

Bearings, 89

Belle Glade site, 50; excavation by Stirling, 156; similar to Fort Center site, 52

Benchmarks (USGS), 85

Big Circle Mounds, 52

Big-game hunting stage. *See* Paleoindian period

Black drink (*Ilex vomitoria*), 43, 108, 180

Body mass (biomass): in determining meat weight, 112-13

Bola stones, 6, *6,* 7, 36

Bolen points, 7, *8,* 9, 10; and end of nomadic lifestyle, 64; Little Salt Spring, 7

Bone: analysis of, 112, *113;* butchering marks on, 5, *5;* decorated, *27;* preservation of, 150; subjective issues, 114-15; as substitute for stone, 26; taphonomy of, 115

Bone beds, controversy over, 63

Bordes, François, 120

Bottle gourds, *108;* use of, 36

Bow and arrow: adoption of, 53-54; Pinellas points and, 49

B.P., definition, 2, 139

Brain tissue. *See* Crania

Bullen, Ripley P.: discussion of theories of, 34-35; summary of Orange period, 34

Bureau of American Ethnology, 155

Bureau of Archaeological Research, 161

Bureau of Historic Preservation, 161

Burials: bundled, 43-44, 50; Cades Pond, 48; changes in practice of, 23; child, at Windover, 18, *18;* customs, 44; destroyed by excavations, 49; Fort Center, 50;

Middle to Late Archaic, 22; radiocarbon dating of, 23; as source of cultural information, 65; variety of, 44-45; Weeden Island, 47; wet sites, 23; Windover, *18;* Yent ceremonial complex, 43. *See also* Charnel houses

Butchering marks, importance of, in dating bones, 5

Buzzard Cult, 53

Cades Pond sites, 48

Cannons, preservation of, 154

Canoes, 34; types of wood used for, 109; from wetsites, *109*

Carbon: in radiocarbon dating, 138, 140

Carbon-14 dating. *See* Radiocarbon dating

Catchment area, 108

Cave-in, prevention of, in excavations, 96, *97*

Cemetery sites. *See* Burials

Central places, 55

Ceramic period, 28-56; dates, 2, 28; differentiated from Archaic, 28; external influences during, 29-34; Mississippian attributes, 53; Mississippian period, 52-56; resulting from sedentism, 36; sites, 50; South Florida, 45; three phases of, 28

Ceramics: curation of, 153; degradation of, 152-53; fiber-tempered, 29-30; importance of, 41; preservation of, 153; standardizing for analysis, 122. *See also* Pottery

Ceramic technologist, information detected by, 121

Chalky ware, St. Johns I, 43

Charnel houses, 43-44, *44,* 48; Fort Center, 50. *See also* Burials; Cades Pond sites

Check-stamped pottery, 54, *55*

Chert: benefits of heating, 13, 118; bifaces and vitreous luster, *14;* changes during heating, 14, 118; color changes on heating, *14,* 118; dating by thermoluminescence, 145; determining composition of, 118-19; fossils in, 118; fossils in identification of, 118; fracture patterns, 116-17, *117;* potlidding (crazing), 117; standards for analysis, 118; use during Middle and Late Archaic, 19; weathering and patina formation, 119-20, 144

Chronology chart, of early cultures of
Florida, 70
Chronometric dating: scarcity for
Paleoindian period, 3, 7; types of, 138-46.
See also Absolute dating
Classification, 116; definition, 1; function
of, 2
Clay: boiling balls, 28-29, 66; coiling for
pottery, 35; identifying sources of, 123;
poorly fired, 153. *See also* Ceramics;
Tempering agents
Climate changes, 64; Archaic period, 11-12
Clovis points, *3;* associated with ancient
elephants, 3-4; dates, 4; in Florida, 4;
lack of, in Florida, 6; unique to
Paleoindian period, 4
Column samples, 101; Hontoon Island, *104;*
reasons for, 103-5
Comparative method, 15, 116, 136-37
Compliance review program, 163; National
Environmental Policy Act (NEPA)
(1969), 159; staff of Bureau of Historic
Preservation, 167
Conservation and Recreation Lands
Program (CARL), 163
Contact, external, 2, 29, 33-34, 35, 52, 56-61
Contour interval (vertical distance), 92
Contour mapping, *93;* example, *90;*
surveying instruments for, 85
Contract archaeology, 158, 164
Copper: in Archaic period, 133; artifacts, 2;
breastplates, *53, 54;* controversial studies
of C. B. Moore, 132-34; in Mississippian
period, 133; origin of, 133; in Pre-
columbian Florida, 131; sources of
artifacts, 134
Coprolites, as evidence for diet, 52, 67, 111
Cordell, Ann S., 122
Corn, controversy over pollen, 52
Corn (*Zea maize*), 28
Crabtree, Don, 120
Crania, 17; Little Salt Spring, 22; Republic
Groves, 22; Vero Beach and Melbourne
Beach bone beds, 63; Warm Mineral
Springs Man, 63
Crazing (potlidding), 117
Crystal River State Archaeological Site, as
example of Yent ceremonial complex, 43
Cucurbita pepo. See Bottle gourds

Cultural change, Late Archaic, 28
Cultural resource management (CRM), 81;
definition, 158-59
Culture Area Concept, 37-38; as applied to
Florida, 39; flaws in, 39
Culture areas, 37; map, *38;* Northwest
Pacific Coast, 38
Curation, 147; of ceramics, 153; of organic
materials, 150-51; of stone artifacts, 152;
tasks in, 151
Cushing, Frank Hamilton, 125-26; repli-
cation of shell artifacts, 126; work at Key
Marco site, 130

Data universe, 81
Dating methods: chert weathering, 144;
chronometric dating, 138-42; comparative, 15, 116, 136, 137; dendrochronology,
140-41; obsidian hydration, 141, 144;
radiocarbon dating, 138-40; stone, 116;
techniques, 116, 120; thermoluminescence, 144-46
Datum plane: definition, 85; determining,
86
Datum point, definition, 85
De Soto, Hernando, 56; excavations related
to, 68-69; route through Florida, 68
Debitage: shell, 127, 128; stone, 21
Degradation: of ceramics, 152-53; of metals,
153; of organic materials, 147-48; of stone
artifacts, 151-52
Dendro-calibration, printout, 141, *142-43*
Dendrochronology, 140-41; accuracy of,
140; A. E. Douglass and, 140; combined
with radiocarbon dating, 141; principles
of, 141
Deposition, of sediments, 9
Deptford (Gulf Coast): connection to
Woodland cultures, 42; food, 42;
pottery, 41-43, 121, 123; pottery as trade
goods, 43; replaced, 45
Development and archaeology, 23, 156
Dewatering system, at Windover site, *16*
Díaz Vara Calderón, Gabriel, 61
Diet: aquatic resources in, 124; Archaic
period, 12; described by Fontaneda, 68;
in determining cultural differences, 114;
evidence of, in pottery, 123; Late Archaic
period, 27; meat weight analysis, 112-14;

plants in, 110-11; shellfish in, 124-25; and social status, 114; of Spanish, 114; strontium analysis of, 114

Diffusion, 37, 41; importance of Gulf Coast in, 37

Direct percussion, 117

Distance, measurement of, in archaeological site, 85-88

Division of Historical Resources: four functional units of, 161; shipwreck salvage policy of, 165-66

Division of Historical Resources (Florida), 158; *The Historic Compliance Review Program,* 160

Division of labor, 37, 66

DNA (deoxyribonucleic acid), 111

Dunns Creek Red pottery, 48

Echo sounding, 80

Ecofacts, 147

Electrical resistivity, 80

Electron spin resonance, 146

Electro-optical distance measuring (EDM), 88

Elephants, extinct: and humans, 4, 138; ivory tools, dating of, 4-5, 62-63; mammoth, 3, *4;* mastodon, 3, 4

Elevation: measurement of, in archaeological site, 85-88, *87;* reasons for recording, 92

Emergency archaeology. *See* Cultural resource management (CRM)

Emergency salvage. *See* Cultural resource management (CRM)

Environmental assessment (EA), 159

Environmental impact statement (EIS), 159

Equipment, for excavation, 93-95

Erosion, exceeding deposition, 10

Ethnocentrism, 57, 115

European explorers: impact on Florida, 56, 69

Eutectic development, 118

Excavations: under adverse conditions, 83; balks, 96-98; benefits from remote sensing, 79-80; box-grid, 96; datum plane for vertical control, 85; datum point for horizontal control, 85; equipment for, 93-95; excavation units (squares), 98-99; features, 101-2; maps for, 76-79; need for information prior to,

81; permits for, 168; by Purdy, 19, 65, 69; quadrant method, 96; screening artifacts, *100,* 100-101; selecting sites for, 84-85; steps in beginning, 75-83, 95-99; stratigraphy, 102-3; systematic, 49; tasks during, 94; trenching, 95-96; uniqueness of each, 83

Executive Order 11593 (1971), 157

Extinction of Ice Age animals, 12

Fairbanks, Charles H., 84

Fauna: analysis of, in archaeological sites, 111-15; associated with humans, 63; MIN, 111, 112; modern, 7

Features: burials as, 102; buried, 80; definition, 101; mapping in planview, 101; recording, 91

Federal Advisory Council on Historic Preservation, 157, 159

Fiber-tempered ceramics, 30

Field methods, 85-99

Flint. *See* Chert

Flintknappers, 13, 116, 120

Flora, 65; analysis of, in archaeological sites, 107-11; corn, 28; corn pollen, 52; uses for, 67

Florida Administrative Code, and shipwreck salvage, 165

Florida Anthropological Society, 163

Florida Archaeological Council, 163

Florida Bureau of Archaeological Research, 164; implementation of training program, 164; Roger C. Smith, 164

Florida Folklife Programs, 161

Florida Historical Resources Act: similar to National Historic Preservation Act (NHPA) (1966), 161

Florida Historical Society, 163

Florida Humanities Council, 163

Florida Museum of Natural History, 168

Florida Program of Vertebrate Paleontology, 168

Florida Site File (FSF), 105, 163; Guidelines for Users, 167-68, *69-70;* Marion Smith, 167; registration of sites, 167

Florida Trust for Historic Preservation, 163

Fontaneda, Escalente: descriptions of Indians' diet, 67; historic accounts, 56, 59-61, 66

Period, definition, 3
Permits, to conduct excavations, 168
pH, definition, 15
Physical anthropologists, 102
Plant Life in Sixteenth Century Florida, 67-68
Plants. *See* Flora
Planviews, 99; and features, 101-2
Pleistocene megafauna, extinction of, in Florida, 5
Pollen analysis (palynology), 110
Polyethylene glycol (PEG), as preservative for wood, 149
Population increases, Ceramic period, 37, 45
Potlidding (crazing), 117
Pottery: check-stamped, 54, *55;* controversy over origins, 29, 66; as cultural marker, 123; Deptford, 42; external influences on, 29-34, 35; Glades Plain, 122-23; introduction of, 18; kill holes, 43; Late Ceramic period, 54; manufacture of, 30, 43, 122-23; Orange series, 30-31; Orange Series as earliest ceramics, 66; Orange Series designs compared, *32;* origins of, 121; paste composition, 122-23; reflecting weaving patterns, 18, *31;* ritual associated with, 122; sand-tempered, 122-23; Savannah, 123; St. Johns I, 43; tempering agents, 35, 121; use of, in dating of sites, 121, 122-23; weaving patterns on, 31; Weeden Island, 122. *See also* Ceramics
Pottery sherds, color differences in, *30*
Pre-Clovis finds, 5
Prentice, Guy, replication experiments, 127-28
Preservation: of ceramics, 153; of metals, 153-54; of organic materials, 148-50; of stone artifacts, 152
Pressure flake, 117
Primary burial method, 45
Probabilistic sampling, 81
Projectile point manufacture: steps in, 116-18; study of steps in, 19
Projectile points: Archaic chert bifaces, *14;* Bolen, 7, *8,* 9, 10, 64; Clovis, 3-4; comparison of, *49;* corner-notched spearheads, 31, *33;* determining age of, 116; as evidence for dating sites, 64; Kirk

Serrated, 15, *16;* Newnans, *20,* 23; Pinellas, 49, 52, *53;* replication of, 120; Simpson, 7, *8,* 9; Suwannee, 7, *8,* 9, 64; Suwannee River, *119*
Proton magnetometer, in locating archaeological sites, 80
Provenience, 23
Purdy, Barbara A., excavations, 19, 62, 65, 69
Pyrotechniques, 121

Quadrangle maps, 76-79; of Alachua County, *77;* of Gainesville, Florida, *78*
Quarry workshop sites, 19, 21, 24, 64, 116-17; abandonment of, 24; as industrial sites, 21; stone debitage, 21; as training sites, 21

Radiocarbon dating: accelerator mass spectrometer and, 140; destructiveness of, 140; discovery of, 138; of fossilized bones, 63; materials to test, 139; meaning of dates, 139; principles of, 138-39
Red ochre (hematite), 44
Regulations, 168. *See also* Laws; Legislation, protective
Relative dating, 136, 137-38; example of, *138*
Remote sensing, 79-80; benefits of, 79-80; need for follow-up, 79
Replication of artifacts: metals, 134-35; shell, 125-29; stone, 120
Rescue archaeology. *See* Cultural resource management (CRM)
Revitalization movements, 61
Revolts, Indian, 61
Rock varnish, 120

Salvage archaeology. *See* Cultural resource management
Sampling: difficulties in, 81; nonprobabilistic, 81; probabilistic, 81; surface collections, 82; techniques, 81-82
Sand mound burials, 43, 48. *See also* Burials; Charnel houses
Sand-tempered Plain pottery (Glades Plain), 122-23
Savannah pottery, 123
Scale, map (horizontal distance), 92
Screening artifacts, 100-101, *101*

Sears, William H.: Fort Center excavations, 50. *See also* Fort Center site
Seasonality as indicator of site occupation, 66, 131
Secondary burial method, 45
Sedentism, resulting from aquatic resources, 36
Seminoles, 2
Seriation of artifacts, 137
Sexagesimal system, in measurement of angles, 89
Shellfish, types utilized, 124
Shells: abundance of, in archaeological sites, 130; analysis of, in archaeological sites, 124-31; degradation of, 148; durability of implements, 128, 129; evidence of, in archaeological sites, 24-25; name changes of species, 131; ornaments of, 26; used as cooking vessels, 24, 126; uses of, 129. *See also* Marine shell technology
Shepard, Anna O., and ceramics standardization, 122
Shipwrecks, 2, 167; ownership of, 165; plundered by Indians, 60; salvage of, 165; as source of European materials, 60
Side-scan sonar, 80
Simpson spearheads, 7, *8*
Sites: Archaic period, 22-25; Paleoindian period, 5, 7, 9; Ceramic period, 30-31, 36, 41-45, 48, 50, 54
Smith, Marion, and Florida Site File (FSF), 167-68
Smith, Roger C., 164
Smithsonian Institution, 155, 156, 157
Soapstone. *See* Steatite
Social status, interpreted from archaeological record, 37, 54, 55
Social structure, Late Ceramic period, 41
Societies, complex: criteria for, in archaeological record, 66-67
Society of Professional Archaeologists (SOPA), 160; standards for culture resource management (CRM), 160
Socketed bone tools. *See* Tools
Solís de Merás, Gonzalo, 29
Southern Cult, 53
South Florida: cemetery sites, 25; Ceramic period, 45; diagnostic flint tools, 25

Spearheads, 2; corner-notched, 31; Kirk Serrated, 15, *16;* styles, Middle and Late Paleoindian, 7; Suwannee, 7, *8*
Spearthrower. *See* Atlatl
Special use sites, 75
St. Augustine, 60; mission, 61
St. Johns I: pottery, 43, 121
St. Johns region: check-stamped pottery, 54; Deptford ceramics, 42; Deptford culture, 45; Late Archaic period, 24, 25, 27; Middle Ceramic period, 35, 36; similarities to Nile region, 41
Stadia rod, in measuring elevation, 85, *87*
Standards: for ceramic analysis, 122-23; for chert analysis, 118; for cultural resource management, 160
State historic preservation officer (SHPO), 157, 159; assisted by SHPO staff, 161
Steatite, 119; beads, *35;* importance of, 35
Stirling, M.W., 156
Stone tools: analysis of, 115-20; manufacturing decline, 24, 31; replication experiments, 120
Stone tools, Archaic: difficulty in classifying, 19-20; multifunctional, 19-20
Stratigraphic profiles, 99
Stratigraphy, 102-3; as dating method, 137; of Hontoon Island site, *103;* Law of Superposition, 103
Strontium, data on, in diet, 114
Sub-bottom profiler, 80
Supplements for Site Forms, 176
Survey data forms, 82-83
Survey Log Sheet, *171*
Surveys, field. *See* Archaeological surveys
Suwannee spearheads, 7, *8*
Swift Creek culture, 45, 46

Taphonomy, 115
Taxonomists, 1
Tempering agents, 30, 35, 121; discovery of, by magnification, 123
Temple mounds, 54, 55
Textiles, Windover site: preservation of, 149-50; uniqueness of, 17-18
Theft of artifacts, 152, 154
Theodolites, in surveying, 88
Thermal alteration. *See* Chert; Heat treatment process

Thermoluminescence: advantages and disadvantages of, 146; as dating method for artifacts, 62, 144-46; as dating method for ceramics, 123; equipment for, 145-46; principles of, 144-45

Tick Island site, 48; Incised pottery, age of, 31

Timucuan Indians, 61; linguistic links, 33; villages of, 58

Tocobaga Indians, 54-55; capture of Juan Ortiz, 54

Tool kit, stone: Late Ceramic period, 39; Middle Archaic, 20; Paleoindian, 10, 10-11

Tools: Archaic period, 15, 16, 21; Paleoindian period, 4-5, 10-11

Topographic maps, 77; significance of, 92

Townships, 77, 78

Trade, and Interaction Sphere, 46-47

Trade goods, Deptford, 42

Training: of archaeologists, 83-84, 86; of law enforcement officers, 164

Transits, in surveying, 85-88

Transit station, use of, 86, 86

Trenching, 95-96, 96

Trust for Public Lands, 163

Typology, 1, 116

Ulna awl, 2

Underwater archaeology, 164, 167

Underwater sites, 75; location of, 80

Unifacial blades, 10

University of Florida, 78, 168

Use wear studies of stone implements, 120

U.S. Geological Survey (USGS), 76

Vernier scale, 88

Wacissa River, 5

Warao language, 33

Warm Mineral Springs Man, 63

Waterlogged sites. See Wetsites

Weathering: of ceramics, 153; of chert, 119, 144; in dating artifacts, 144; experiments, 62; patina in, 119-20, 144; rock varnish, 120; types of, 119-20

Weeden Island site, 45-48; effigy vessel, 46; as multicenter model, 122; relative dates, 46

Wetherill, Richard, 156

Wet sites: Archaic period, 15; human burials, 23; Lake Monroe, 30; map, 21; preservation, 23, 108, 108

Willey, Gordon R., and theory of remote contact , 47

Windover site, 11; cultural information from, 17; dates for, 15-16, 64; excavations, 16; grave goods, 18; Kirk Serrated spearhead, 15, 16; as landmark site, 16; organic material artifacts, 17, 17-18; preservation of textiles, 149-50; projectile points, 15, 16, 64; uniqueness of, 17-19; wooden artifacts, 17

Wood: analysis of, 110; artifacts as definition of regional cultures, 39; artifacts from Fort Center site, 50; artifacts from Late Ceramic period, 40; identification of, by wood anatomist, 110; selection of, by Indians, 108-9

Wood, waterlogged, preservation of, 149-50

Works Progress Administration (WPA) and role in archaeological excavations, 156

Xeroradiography, 134-35

Yent ceremonial complex: burials, 43

Zooarchaeologist, information detected by, 111

Zooarchaeology, 111